Starve
State Park

The First 100 Years

MARK WALCZYNSKI

Outskirts Press, Inc.
Denver, Colorado

Starved Rock State Park
The First 100 Years

v4.0

Outskirts Press, Inc.
http://www.outskirtspress.com

ISBN: 978-1-4327-7610-7

PRINTED IN THE UNITED STATES OF AMERICA

Contents

Preface

The purpose of this book is to give the reader a very, very brief look at some of the events that have occurred at Starved Rock State Park since the year 1911. But before I get to 1911, I thought that it would be a good idea to give a very short background history of the site including the geologic story of how today's Starved Rock was formed, the French and Native American history, and some events leading up to the site's purchase by the State of Illinois. This work is a simple narrative that moves quickly through time with a few incidents and anecdotes highlighted along the way. Some readers might be disappointed that I did not spend enough time covering certain aspects of park history, such as the fine work done at the park by the Civilian Conservation Corps (CCCs). Others might be disappointed that I made no mention of the Starved Rock murders, a terrible incident that occurred at the park (St. Louis Canyon) in 1960. Although I understand these concerns, it should be pointed out that the role of the CCCs at Starved Rock and details of the infamous murder case have been well documented in a variety of books, films, and presentations. Likewise, I am sure that some readers will feel that I have spent far too much time on insignificant periods and events. But again, this little book was meant only to be a guide to park visitors who know little about the park itself and the history of its times. Hopefully the reader will get a little better appreciation of the park by seeing how things came to be what they are today. And, hopefully the pictures that accompany this narrative will demonstrate that Starved Rock State Park is an evolving work in progress with much more to come.

Due to the sensitive nature of certain State of Illinois correspondences, some names have been changed to protect the identity of the people involved.

Acknowledgements

This book could have not been written without the encouragement of the Board of Directors of the Starved Rock Historical and Educational Foundation and the helpful staff of Starved Rock State Park who gave me access to their extensive cache of park documents and photos. I would like to thank Carleen Skerston and Roger "Buck" Harbeck for their time and for sharing a few of their fond memories of the park with me. I would like to thank Ed Jelks, the last professional archaeologist to excavate the summit of Starved Rock, for giving me insight into his work at the site. I would also like to thank two of Illinois' hardest working librarians, Donna and Brittany Blomquist of the La Salle Public Library, for locating and sorting through volumes of documents, newspaper articles, and books. These two ladies certainly made my job much easier. And finally, I would like to thank my friend and colleague Michael McCafferty, of Indiana University, and Foundation member John Muir (yes, that's his real name) for reviewing and commenting on my manuscript.

Introduction

Today's Starved Rock State Park has a wonderful history. Our story begins during the last Ice Age, when today's Canada and the northern United States were covered by immense sheets of ice called glaciers. These glaciers, sometimes a mile thick, acted like giant snow plows, pushing rock, rubble, and debris southward. When the temperatures warmed, the ice sheets receded, and when the temperatures cooled again, they continued plowing their way south. This plowing action of the glaciers piled large mounds of dirt and debris called moraines, "C" shaped hills that extend for several miles. Moraines are noticeably visible throughout the corn country of Illinois, just look for the newly constructed wind turbines—most of them are built on glacial moraines.

Eventually, temperatures warmed and the glaciers began to melt. As a consequence, water from melting glaciers left ponds and lakes, similar to those seen in Canada and northern Midwestern states. In addition, the vast amount of water trapped behind the moraines (the Great Lakes had not yet been formed) eventually broke through and inundated the landscape, washing away vast stretches of land. This torrent of water, sometimes called the "Kankakee Torrent," carved out the Upper Illinois Valley. It also washed away the land that was once between today's Starved Rock and the bluff south of it. Starved Rock became an erosional remnant of pre-Ice Age Illinois.

About 10,000 years ago, roughly 3,000 years after the torrent carved out the Upper Illinois Valley, Native Americans moved into the Starved Rock region. These people left remnants of their technology including projectile points (commonly called "arrowheads"), scrapers, and assorted tools. From that early period onward until today, the Starved Rock area has been nearly continuously inhabited by Man. Assorted artifacts of stone, bone, shell, and clay are testament to the area's occupation by Indians of the Archaic, Woodland, and Mississippian cultural traditions.

The written record of early Illinois and the Starved Rock region did not begin until 1673, when a French expedition that included Jesuit missionary Jacques Marquette, fur trader and businessman Louis Jolliet (yes, Jolliet has two "L"s) and five other Frenchmen passed today's Starved Rock while traveling north on their "Voyage of Discovery." Although Marquette never specifically mentioned Starved Rock in his official report of the expedition, he did note the beauty and fertility of the Illinois Valley;

> "We have seen nothing like this river that we enter, as regards its fertility of soil, its prairies and woods; its cattle, elk, deer, wildcats, bustards, swans, ducks, parroquets, and even beaver. There are many small lakes and rivers. That on which we sailed is wide, deep, and still, for 65 leagues. In the spring and during part of the summer there is only one portage of half a league."

Marquette also wrote that his party stopped at a Kaskaskia Indian village (the Kaskaskia were an Illinois Indian sub-tribe) that was located about a mile upstream from the Rock and on the other side of the river. The missionary noted that the village consisted of seventy-four "cabins" and that the Kaskaskia people "received us very well."

Explorer Louis Jolliet as portrayed in
the Starved Rock Visitor's Center.

Another Jesuit missionary, Claude-Jean Allouez, visited the Kaskaskia village at times between 1677 and 1679. Among many things, he noted that the Illinois Indians who lived there ate "14 different kinds of roots; from the trees and plants they gather 42 different of fruits, and catch 25 sorts of fish; hunt 22 kinds of large animals; and forty different kinds of game and birds," a testament to nature's bounty in seventeenth century Illinois.

On January 1, 1680, the expedition of René-Robert Cavalier Sieur de La Salle arrived in the Starved Rock area and stopped at the Kaskaskia village. Three months later, La Salle wrote the first historical reference to Starved Rock in orders issued to his second in command, Henri Tonti: "go to the old village [the Illinois Indian village upstream from Starved Rock] to visit a rock" and "build a strong fort upon it." Although Tonti was unable to carry out La Salle's orders at this time, a fort was constructed on today's Starved Rock during the winter of 1682 and 1683. This fort, dubbed, Fort Saint-Louis (after Louis IX, *a.k.a.* Saint Louis) was built under the supervision of Jacques Bourdon d'Autray. The fort became the headquarters for what history calls "La Salle's Colony," a gathering of an estimated 20,000 Native Americans (Illinois, Miami, Shawnee, and others) who lived between today's Utica, Illinois and the confluence of the Kankakee and Des Plaines Rivers. In April 1683, Illinois' first land grant was awarded to d'Autray for his supervision of the construction of Fort Saint-Louis. D'Autray's land grant began about three miles downstream from the Rock, and continued just east of it. Most of this grant is within the geographical boundaries of today's Starved Rock State Park.

Little Rock, the site where the first land grant in Illinois was awarded to Jacques Bourdon d'Autray in 1683

Another notable event that occurred at Starved Rock during the French occupation of the region happened in March of 1684 when the fort was besieged by two-hundred Iroquois Indians for six days.

The fort's forty-six defenders (24 Frenchmen, 8 Miami, 9 Mohegan, and 5 Shawnee warriors) were, in the words of the forts commandant Henri-Louis Baugy, "all very much resolved to defend us to death." The siege ended when the vanguard of "Colony Indians" returning from the winter hunt overwhelmed the Iroquois with superior numbers and drove them off.

A letter for help written during the Iroquois siege of Fort Saint Louis on March 24, 1684 by Henri-Louis Baugy.

[illegible]

[illegible] tant que les Iroquois [illegible]
[illegible] vous nous envoyez [illegible] faites mettre un escrit au [illegible]
[illegible] ce qu'y [illegible] face [illegible] a [illegible] quel [illegible]
[illegible] tousjours sur ses gardes [illegible]
[illegible] plustost que l'ennemy [illegible] les sauvages
[illegible] un [illegible] par [illegible] village [illegible]
[illegible] que vous nous envoyerez [illegible] leur arrivée [illegible]
[illegible] sauvages [illegible] dont nous vous [illegible]
ayant [illegible] le monde [illegible] les sauvages ne [illegible]
[illegible] nouvelles au plustost [illegible] vous [illegible] tres humble et tres ob[illegible]
[illegible] mon[illegible] [illegible] ces deux mots [illegible] de mes tres humbles [illegible]
[illegible] tous les francois [illegible] de la nation [illegible]
[illegible] pour nous [illegible]
[illegible] l'original
[illegible] le 21.e avril 1684 [illegible]

C'est un extrait de l'original de la
lettre de Mr le chevalier de Baugy
que je certifie estre veritable [illegible]
[illegible]
Henry [illegible]

Depuis cette lettre [illegible] nous avons [illegible] par des sauvages [illegible] des plus braves des
Iroquois demandaient a [illegible] ce qu'on leur accorda sans armes [illegible]
[illegible] y furent [illegible] en pieces [illegible] leurs [illegible]
[illegible] la [illegible] et quatre [illegible] la plainte
[illegible] Baugy [illegible]
[illegible] les [illegible]
[illegible] un sauvage [illegible]
[illegible]
[illegible]

On a side note, the United States Navy commissioned the USS La Salle, an amphibious transport vessel and command ship that operated in the Middle Eastern theater between 1972 and 2005. The USS La Salle (also known as the "Great White Ghost of the Arabian Coast," or the "Great White Target" because of its painted white exterior and lack of guns), was instrumental in the evacuation of two-hundred-sixty "American and foreign national civilians" during the Iranian Hostage Crisis. On the ship's crest was the coat of arms of the La Salle family and an image of Fort Saint-Louis, La Salle's fort on top of today's Starved Rock.

Bell of the USS La Salle at the La Salle, Illinois City Hall

The French abandoned their fort on Starved Rock in the autumn of 1691 after the Illinois left their village (Kaskaskia village) and established new camps on today's Lake Peoria. The immediate Starved Rock area was uninhabited until 1712 when one band of Peoria Indians (another Illinois Indian sub-tribe) established new camps near Starved Rock. In 1722, the other Peoria band united with the first group of Peoria for protection from marauding Fox Indian war parties that were active in the Illinois Valley. During this time the two Peoria bands lived on Plum Island, the large island directly in front of Starved Rock State Park.

In 1722, a large Fox war party led by the aging chief Ouashala attacked the Peoria camp. Likely roused from their sleep before daylight by the sound of gunshots and war whoops, the Peoria fled the island, ran across the shallow south river channel, and climbed to the summit of the Rock for safety. After a short siege, the Fox and Peorias agreed to a negotiated settlement. The Peorias left the Starved Rock area and moved next to other Illinois sub-tribes (Cahokia and Tamaroa) who lived along the Mississippi River in Southern Illinois. The Fox also left the Rock and headed for home in today's Wisconsin. Later that year, Ouashala, reported to the French at Green Bay and gave his version of the attack on the Peoria village. The chief told the French that he "pressed them [the Peoria] very hard, and it depended only upon myself to carry out my project fully; for, finding themselves on the verge of destruction, reduced by hunger, and deprived of all means of getting water, so that they were beginning to die of thirst." Just how much, if any, of Ouashala's account was embellished is difficult to determine. What we do know is that the 1722 Fox siege of the Peorias at the Rock became the basis for the famous legend of the nineteenth century.

Eight years later, some Peoria and a few Cahokia (another subtribe of the Illinois Indians) were living the Starved Rock area. Again, these Illinois skirmished with the Fox Indians, an episode that ended several months later at the horrific siege of the Fox fort, a site believed by many researchers to have been near today's Arrowsmith, Illinois, McLean County. The last known credible historical reference to the Illinois Indians at the Rock is in 1751.

Starved Rock gets its name from an incident that allegedly occurred at the site in 1769. According to the well-known legend, an Illinois Indian killed the famous war chief Pontiac either in southern Illinois or at today's Joliet. As a consequence, Pontiac's Indian allies including the Potawatomi and Ottawa (and according to some accounts the Miami, Kickapoo, and Winnebago warriors) attacked Illinois villages and drove the survivors to the summit of the Rock. There the Illinois Indians found themselves hopelessly surrounded by their enemies with no avenue of escape. Eventually, as the story goes, the Illinois died from starvation on the summit or were massacred below while attempting to escape. Although the legend is a tragic tale of bloodshed and revenge, there is no credible written or archaeological evidence to substantiate it, and there is much period documentation to refute it.

Starved Rock as seen from the Illinois River.

The departure of the Illinois Indians from the Illinois Valley (and the northern part of the state) created a void that was soon filled by the Potawatomi. The Potawatomi established villages on the Illinois River between Starved Rock and today's Peoria, on the Fox, Kankakee, and lower Des Plaines Rivers (at the Forks), and along other small watercourses such as today's Indian Creek (south De Kalb and north La Salle Counties).

British presence in the Upper Illinois Valley occurred in 1773 when a British geological expedition led by Patrick Kennedy passed

Starved Rock while searching for copper. The Americans arrived in the area in 1789 when a U.S. Army expedition charged with mapping the Illinois River passed the "Small Rocks," Starved Rock and the adjacent bluffs and rapids. In 1821 geologist, Indian agent, and ethnographer Henry Schoolcraft visited a place he called "Rockfort," today's Starved Rock. In 1835, Starved Rock's first private American owner, Daniel Hitt, reportedly purchased Starved Rock and adjacent property (a total of sixty-eight acres) from the United States government for $85.00. Hitt, a Black Hawk and Civil War veteran and La Salle County's first surveyor owned the property until 1890, when he sold it to Chicago businessman Ferdinand Walther. Walther owned Starved Rock and adjacent properties for twenty-one years. Walther's tenure of ownership includes opening the property to the public as a private park and constructing the Starved Rock Hotel and nearby cabins to house visitors.

The Starved Rock Hotel, early 1900s

In 1911, the State of Illinois purchased the property from Walther. The site became Starved Rock State Park, Illinois' second state park (Fort Massac was the first in 1908). Besides hiking and sight seeing, the park is a splendid place to camp, picnic, go fishing, rent a canoe, launch a boat, observe nature, or just relax. The park has a wonderful visitor's center that sells an assortment of nature and history books and some hiking paraphernalia. The volunteers of the Starved Rock Educational and Historical Foundation lead guided hikes on week-ends and offer programs for kids and adults. The Starved Rock lodge is complete with shops, restaurant, a bar, and at times, entertainment. Satellite sites of the park include both Matthiessen State Parks (Dells and Vermilion River Area), the Sandy Ford Conservation area, Miller Woods Conservation area, and various nature preserves. Starved Rock State Park and its satellite parks is a great place to learn and enjoy nature.

1
The Early Years

During the latter years of the 19th and early years of the 20th century, a public effort was afoot to preserve land for public use and safekeeping from development. The wild spaces of America's frontier had nearly all been conquered and the need to save the parts of it that remained was an important matter, especially for sake of future generations. This effort to save some of our dwindling resources, sometimes called the "Conservation Movement," was the impetus for national acquisition of many parks such as Yellowstone and other refuge areas. By 1912, the federal government had reportedly purchased "four million acres in thirteen different localities" for public ownership (some of these sites included Yosemite, Crater Lake, Sequoia, and Glacier National Parks).

On the state level, there was a similar effort to acquire and preserve land. Leading states in this endeavor included New York, California, Massachusetts, and Wisconsin. Following the lead of these states were Michigan (to obtain Mackinac Island), Ohio (Fort Ancient, Serpent Mound, etc.), Minnesota, New Jersey, and Kansas. This same attitude was the force that drove conservation minded citizens through their elected officials to purchase unique places such as Starved Rock. Influential private citizens and politicians in Chicago and across the state began mobilizing, appealing to "some of our more patriotic organizations in Illinois" to join the effort for the state purchase of Starved Rock.

One of these local influential citizens was Eaton Osman of Ottawa. In 1895, Osman wrote a book entitled, "Starved Rock: A Chapter of Colonial History." Osman's book was the textbook for the history of Starved Rock at that time, and copies of it were used to woo and "pressure" prospective state legislators to join the campaign for the purchase of the park. Public interest in the history of Starved Rock as reported by Osman continued to grow for the next few years. On April 19, 1910, Osman delivered a lecture to the Chicago Historical Society proclaiming La Salle's Fort Saint-Louis as the "Keystone" of the empire of New France. He spoke about of the role of Tonti (La Salle's second in command) and the role of the Illinois Indians during the French occupation of the Starved Rock area. Osman also described the region's Indian wars, and he relayed to his audience the Legend of Starved Rock. A particular point of interest is that Osman's "Starved Rock" book was renamed and republished in 1923 and called "The Last of a Great Indian Tribe"—same book, different title.

Other influential societies also kept interest in the "Starved Rock proposition" alive. The Geographic Society of Chicago, for example, held a "Special Program" on Friday evening, April 22, 1910 at the Chicago Art Institute whose agenda for the evening included a presentation by Dr. Wallace W. Atwood entitled Starved Rock and the Canyons of the Illinois. The technology of the day was featured at the event, as an advertisement for it read "each number on the program will be fully illustrated with the stereopticon." The Catholic Church was also requested to join the effort for state purchase of Starved Rock. In a letter to Paul Blatchford (Chairman of the Committee of the Starved Rock reservation, dated Dec. 10, 1908) an inquiry was made to see "if some of the societies of the Catholic Church would be willing to work for the plan." Another behind-the-scene organization that pushed for state ownership of the park was the Daughters of the American Revolution (DAR). It was reported that Mrs. John C. Ames and Mrs. Frank B. Orr of the DAR knew the Illinois State Park Commissioners, and with the help of many Illinois DAR members could "induce" the Illinois State Legislature to appropriate funds for purchase of the park and for general maintenance.

CHICAGO HISTORICAL SOCIETY

DEARBORN AVENUE AND ONTARIO STREET.

A Special Meeting of the CHICAGO HISTORICAL SOCIETY
will be held in the Society's Building,
Tuesday Evening, April 19, 1910,
at eight o'clock, when

EATON G. OSMAN

will deliver a lecture, entitled:

"STARVED ROCK: A CHAPTER OF COLONIAL HISTORY,
1663-1730."

Members and their friends are invited to be present.

FRANKLIN H. HEAD,
PRESIDENT.

SYNOPSIS: LaSalle builds Ft. St. Louis as the Keystone of the Empire of New France—Tonty and the Illinois as the Saviors of New France, 1687—Starved Rock the Wedge, and the Foxes the Sledge, to destroy New France—Tonty the Father of Louisiana—Planting the Seeds of Christianity in the Mississippi Valley—The last stand of the Peorias and the "Starved Rock Legend."

Mr. Osman is a native of LaSalle County and has had exceptional opportunities for investigating the locality.

The program for Eaton Osman's lecture to the Chicago Historical Society April 19, 1910

In 1911, the State of Illinois purchased the property that became Starved Rock State Park. Although the park officially opened for business under state authority on May 1, 1911, negotiations for the price and extent of the property between the park's private owner, Ferdinand Walther, and the State of Illinois did not begin until September 20. On September 22, Walther agreed to accept $150,000.00 for the land and buildings. But before the deal could be finalized, the state insisted that an audit of Walther's books be conducted by "prominent bankers, bond brokers, and hotel owners." According to the bankers, the property was worth $146,428.00. The bond brokers believed that the price should be somewhat less and the hotel owners believed that the price should be considerably higher. An agreement was eventually reached between the two parties for the 280 acres of land originally bartered for and an additional 10 acres of woodland "lying outside of the reservation." The price tag was $146,000.000. The state also purchased 6.04 acres from the Hitt/Russell estate (adjacent to today's Starved Rock boat ramp area) for $875.00 and additional 18.59 acres for $2,665.00.

Although the deal for the property had been finalized, there was no budget for a park. Monies for park maintenance, employee salaries, and other obligations had not yet been appropriated. To meet state expenses, a state-run concession for the sale of post cards and souvenirs was established and guides were furnished for visitors who desired them. But what about the administration and operation of the Starved Rock Hotel, park cottages, concessions (ice cream and candies being specifically mentioned), farm leases, entertainment facilities (bowling alley and dance hall), pleasure boats, and liveries and ferries? The Illinois State Park Commission determined that proprietorship of the park concessions must be open for public bidding, and soon.

However, local businessmen had no idea of how much to bid for park concessions as "there were no actual figures on which to base returns." There was also the problem with the ferry that transported visitors from the north side of the river to the park (located on the south side of the river) in that, when Walther sold the land to the state, he no longer operated the ferry service. And, there were concerns about the funds, or lack thereof, needed to maintain the park. To the latter concern the Commission decided that concessionaires would have to pay for the upkeep of park grounds.

The park's new infrastructure had to be improved to meet the anticipated thousands of new visitors. Roads had to be graded, repaired, and reopened and a parking lot had to be built. An artificial lake on park property that had broken out from its banks needed to be drained and the water diverted to the river. The artesian well and water system needed overhauling. During the preparation process, work crews would also have to remove dead trees, stumps, and branches and burn what would be an estimated four hundred wagon loads of debris.

Rules for public use of Illinois parks were also written. Some of the ordinances include prohibitions against willfully destroying, damaging, or defacing any guidepost, sign, or enclosure that was erected for the purposes of "protection or ornament." Violations of these laws included a fine of up to $500.00, up to three months in jail, and/or any combination thereof. The park's flora (plants and plant life) was protected from anyone who "willfully destroys cuts, breaks, injures, or removes any tree, shrub or plant." A ticket for this violation could net the perpetrator a fine between $10.00 and $100.00. And, you will pay your fine! The violator reportedly "shall stand committed to the county jail until such fine and costs are paid." Enforcement of these statutes was the duty of the park superintendent, guardians, and custodians. These officers, forerunners of today's Illinois Conservation Police, were vested with police powers to enforce all state laws on park property. Specifically, these duties fell to Illinois Park Commission member Alexander Richards and "Officer" P.H. Harbeck. Harbeck not only enforced state laws on Starved Rock property, he sometimes also doubled as the "sheriff at Starved Rock" (star number 666) for park guests. Dressed in the uniform of a "bobby" style policeman, Harbeck posed for photos and sometimes helped campers locate a good campsite.

Despite a less than hoped-for turnout, the bid process for park concessions went forward. Accordingly, the hotel, cabin, and dining room concession was awarded to Charles Touton of Peru, Illinois. Touton was responsible for the main floor of the hotel which at the time consisted of offices, two dining rooms, and a kitchen. There were also sleeping quarters on the second floor of the building, which included two double and ten single rooms. On the third floor were two double and three single rooms. The hotel annex included sixteen single rooms, eight of them with baths. The second floor of the hotel's club house consisted of one double and twelve single rooms, while the third floor had four double and four single rooms, the single rooms being used for hotel employees. Of the four cabins, two had three rooms each and two had two rooms each. The larger of the hotel's two dining rooms could hold eighty-five people while the smaller one accommodated fifty-six. The agreement between Touton and the state included provisions that prohibited the sale of "malt, vinous, or spirituous liquors," and prohibited "hogs, cows, or anything of an offensive nature" to be allowed on the premises. Prices were to be plainly posted and could not be changed without the approval of the Illinois Park Commission. Touton agreed to pay the $1,000.00 for rent the first year, $1,200 for the second, and $1,500.00 for the third. It appears that Touton held the concession of the hotel until 1918, when W.E. Crosier secured the site concession.

The Starved Rock Hotel and complex

The concession for the Starved Rock livery and auto bus "privilege" went to Thomas Manley of Utica. Manley was responsible for "operating liveries or automobiles between Utica and Starved Rock and Deer Park and Starved Rock." In addition, "All calls for livery service from the hotel or for conveyances to transport parties to and from the different nearby resorts will be sent to the person holding this concession."

One hundred and thirty acres of tillable park farm ground went to P.H. Harbeck (also listed as an enforcement officer at the park) "upon a basis of two-fifths of the crop, this two-fifths not to be less than $7.00 per acre." Seven acres of ground on one of the islands at Starved Rock went to James Mitchell for twenty dollars per year.

Seven acres of State of Illinois farm concession ground on an island above Starved Rock.

Another important park concession was the first floor of the park's club house which included the "dance hall, bowling alley, ice cream parlor, sleeping apartment and porches, and the 'fountain stand' located between the hotel and the club house." This concession was awarded to W.E. Crosier of Utica. In addition to keeping books that listed expenditures and receipts, "disreputable" people were not allowed to frequent his concession. His concession was to be closed at a "reasonable hour," meaning no later than 11:00 pm—that is unless special permission had been previously granted.

The Starved Rock Hotel built in 1891 had been in business for nearly twenty years by the time the state assumed ownership. With new management came the desire to breathe new life into the old inn. Renovation of the building began but was not completed by the time the park was opened. In fact, it was two weeks afterward that visitors could rent a room, and nearly a month before all concessions were in full operation. To encourage attendance at the park, the state waived the entrance fee. This, it was hoped, "insured in itself the patronage of many additional thousands over previous years."

So how did visitors get to Starved Rock State Park? During the early years of the park, most visitors who traveled a hundred miles or more did so by train, a few of them by auto. Park visitors who arrived by train, were usually taken by the "interurban" rail from the Utica train station to a rail station across the river from the park. From there, a ferry would convey visitors across the Illinois River and to the park. But Walther was no longer operating the ferry. He quit running it when he sold his park to the state. The state therefore entered into contract with the Starved Rock Transportation Company who purchased Walther's boats and operated the tour boat concession at the park. Ferry rates were fifteen cents for a round-trip and ten cents for a one-way crossing. The company also agreed to run a light and power line from Utica to the park. Another project designed to facilitate the anticipated increase in park attendance included construction of a swing bridge across the Illinois River that connected the road between Utica and the park. Built by the War Department, the new bridge allowed vehicular traffic to cross the river and when it swung open, it allowed large boats and passenger vessels that came from the Lower Illinois and Mississippi Rivers to land at the park.

The park's rich history became the subject of film makers and visual performers. During the summer of 1912, sixty to seventy-five cast members, staff, and crew of the American Film Company of Chicago set up camp (on the bluff where today's Starved Rock Lodge stands) to recreate the adventures of French explorers La Salle, Tonti, Jolliet, and Marquette. News of the filming spread throughout the neighborhood of Starved Rock. Reportedly, thousands of people came to the park to watch the historical reenactments and to "enlighten themselves relative to the making of moving pictures." The company also recreated and filmed the Battle of New Orleans. It was reported that the films produced at the park would be seen at about 3,000 "play houses" in the U.S. and Europe.

Starved Rock State Park taken in May 1911. P.H. Harbeck in the center of photo wearing the badge.

The park was open for business, though not year-round as it is today. In 1912, one year after the park was open under state management, the site boasted 75,000 visitors, a considerable increase in attendance when compared to the annual 25,000 people who visited the park when it was under private ownership. The park management and concessionaires could boast that their financial venture into the unknown was a success. It was so much of a success that hotels in the area could not keep up with the demand for lodging. As a consequence, construction of inns and hotels to accommodate the wave of sightseers and guests began in earnest. The days of a leisurely Sunday drive to Starved Rock State Park and the return ride home the same day had not yet arrived. Park visitors at this time needed a place to get a good meal or two and find a place to spend a couple of nights in order to truly enjoy the park.

In September 1913, the Illinois Daughters of the American Revolution (DAR) came to Starved Rock to dedicate a flag staff, five flags and a pennant to the State of Illinois in memory of those soldiers and sailors who had given their lives during the American Revolution and War of 1812. Since the ladies of the DAR influenced state lawmakers to fund the purchase the park, they believed it was "fitting" to donate a one hundred-foot tall flag pole to be placed on the Rock's summit. The dedication ceremony was attended by DAR members from across Illinois, including Honorary President General Mrs. Matthew T. Scott and Vice President General, Mrs. John C. Ames. Other attendees included, for the Governor of Illinois Edward Dunne, Charles F. Clyne (State Representative and later US Attorney for Northern Illinois), Alexander Richards (Illinois Park Commission member), L.Y. Sherman and J. Hamilton Lewis (US Senators), and local historian Eaton Osman. During the ceremony, Osman spoke about the French colonial and Native American history of Starved Rock.

When workers were digging the ten-foot deep foundation hole for the flag staff, they uncovered several Indian "relics" which allegedly included a calumet. The items were then later placed in the foundation hole and covered in cement. At the ceremony, one of the speakers noted that "At the base of this staff several feet under ground was found a calumet or pipe of peace—the most sacred belonging to the savage race. At the top of this staff will float the most sacred belonging of the American people, their symbol of peace, unity, and justice—our flag."

Another outdoor gala was celebrated at the Rock in 1918. This "pageant," reported as the "biggest crowd ever" at Starved Rock wherein all previous attendance records were "shattered," was the one-hundredth anniversary celebration of Illinois statehood. Newspaper accounts reported that no fewer than 20,000 people attended the festivities. Chicago newspapers sent photographers to the gala, the Pathé Company took motion pictures of it, and one-hundred-two "young ladies from La Salle County" donned costumes and represented the one-hundred-two counties of the state. Dignitaries from all over Illinois including Wallace Rice, the composer of our state song, "Illinois," attended the affair. There were also appearances by Abraham Lincoln, Stephen Douglas, Ulysses S. Grant, Jacques Marquette, Louis Jolliet, Cavalier de La Salle, and Henri Tonti—impersonators of course. The local Native American community was represented by a group who portrayed the Illinois Indians and by a Chief Pontiac impersonator. And for the students of nature and metaphysics, no celebration would have been complete without an appearance by Love (Mrs. Sharp), Harmony (Miss Louis Bedford), Rhythm (Miss Gertrude Olmstead), Wisdom (Lloyd Painter), Law (Rev. W.A. Sims), Truth (William Zwanzig), and Common Sense (James O'Toole).

Large outdoor celebrations were not uncommon in the early days at Starved Rock. In 1873 there was a large outdoor gala that celebrated the two-hundredth anniversary of the Jolliet/Marquette expedition that passed today's Starved Rock in late summer of 1673.That celebration boasted, according to one account, between five to six thousand people and like the 1913 DAR dedication, it included an appearance by a well-known local historian, Perry Armstrong. Armstrong dazzled the crowd that day by retelling the story that an elderly Ottawa Indian chief named Shick-Shack told him forty years earlier. According to Armstrong, Shick-Shack not only claimed to have been at the alleged 1769 siege of Illinois Indians at Starved Rock, he said that he led the allied attack on the trapped Illinois. Although Armstrong's colorful tale was told in the beautiful style of the middle nineteenth century, a critical evaluation of it reveals that the story he told the crowd was not only implausible, it was contrary to the well documented period historical record.

2

The Roaring Twenties

Not only did the park attract visitors from all over of Illinois and other states, it was also a place where local people had fun. During this time, the park dance pavilion was one of the most popular places around—a great place to have good clean fun. So clean in fact that certain types of dances were expressly forbidden, like the "shimmy" and "tickle toe." Prohibitions included "Head to head and cheek to cheek dancing" and "fancy steps." Dancers were warned not to "exaggerate any dance," and to make sure they dance "in the same direction." Everyone was reminded, "Please remember this is a state park, and the rules must be obeyed."

During Labor Day weekend of 1923, Starved Rock welcomed an estimated 50,000 people, according to Site Custodian J.P. White. The park's forty-five acre campground was filled to over capacity. Late arrivals had to camp along county roads and on private farms near the park. White also said that over 10,000 cars filled "two-thirds of the 105-acre parking ground at the park, the largest in the state." It was also reported that all area hotel rooms were full by 4:00 pm the Saturday of the holiday weekend. Even private residences opened their doors to the hoard of visitors destined to explore the park. Local businesses reportedly hired extra help and quadrupled supplies of food. The City of Ottawa hired nine additional traffic officers who "worked day and night and helped direct the huge throngs about the city without a single bad accident." On roads leading to Ottawa, extra state patrol officers as well as special deputies were on duty in order to keep the flow of traffic moving. One problem area of highway locally known as "Dimmick Hill" (located today on Illinois Route 71, about three and one half miles east of Illinois Route 178) was patrolled by Trooper Terry Martin (who later became park custodian) and several other officers. It was reported that they kept traffic moving, although slowly.

A park visitor on the summit of Starved Rock circa 1924.

But even with the high volume of park visitors and great work done by traffic authorities and local businesses, there were complaints that the management of the park labored under a different set of priorities than the average park visitor. One such complaint lodged in 1922 lamented, "The Park has never offered any conveniences for the public above the bare necessities except with a fee attached, and, in fact, the whole layout from the time of its acquirement by the state has seemed to be an effort to provide means for someone to make 'a piece of money.' In short, the park has followed the pace set by most of the public outing places and has been commercialized to the limit." The writer believed that the park should provide, without cost, facilities for "picnickers and tourists who may desire to enjoy a state park without expense," rather than spending funds "making the concessions more profitable." To some, the public perception was that the park was nothing more than a hotel and concessions with a piece of state property around them. According to the editorial, other than French Canyon (located about four-tenths of a mile from today's visitor center) the park remains "inaccessible," and as such makes viewing the other canyons and cliffs a "hardship few will undertake." To remedy this problem it was suggested that trail work should begin at once and a comprehensive guide book should be written that provides visitors "a good idea of what there is to be seen and how to get there." In sum, the editorial writer and a few others believed that the park should have the public welfare in mind, not the concessionaires'.

Ironically, five days before the previous editorial was published, Colonel Miller, director of Public Works and Buildings, announced that park improvements were forthcoming. He said that fifty benches and tables would be purchased for public use and that a new drinking water hydrant would be installed. Miller said that, although the Department of Public Works and Buildings had been very busy with road repair, ground maintenance, and building projects at other state sites, he had had the Starved Rock site checked and scrutinized. He admitted that "some of the things that are lacking and are necessary [at Starved Rock] certainly astonish me." About the question concerning the profits made by concessionaires he said, "I want it distinctly understood to start out with the park is not run for the benefit of any one man, or any number of men, but for the public of the state of Illinois."

Even back in the 1920s, operating and maintaining a state owned park was a challange. Before certain kinds of work could be performed, architects had to be consulted, plans had to be drawn, and specifications had to be made. When those steps were completed, the bid process began wherein contractors around the state studied the plans and offered a bid to do the work. Once the bids had been accepted, they were scrutinized by state officials and a determination was made as to which bid offered the best deal for the state. When that process was completed, the requested work was performed. This could be a rather lengthy process.

Work that could be done without having to go through the bid process, however, was done immediately or was at the discretion of the site manager. Some of these projects included building an additional toilet facility, improving the lighting, and constructing "brick ovens" in the campground. Trees cut during these repairs were cut into firewood to be used by campers. But, despite these improvements, there was still eye toward the rustic and natural. Miller believed that to preserve the park's natural beauty, walking bridges on the trails should be constructed of logs with the bark still attached.

A rustic bridge in Horseshoe Canyon.

In response to the previous editorial complaint that there was no park guide book, the state published "What to See and How to See Starved Rock State Park" (1924). The guide was written by Horace Hull of nearby Ottawa under the supervision of the Department of Public Works and Buildings. Inside were pictures of the park including Lover's Leap, the Auto Tourists Shelter House, Horseshoe Canyon, French Canyon, Council Cave, a view from the campground, and pictures of happy park visitors. The guide also contained a brief history of Starved Rock; points of interest; trails to hike with distances included; concessions and services; how to access the park by rail, auto and ferry; and admonitions for fire safety. At a cost of only five cents, the book was a complete guide to Starved Rock State Park.

A primitive campsite in the Starved Rock Campground.

The time and effort spent by Col. Miller and park staff, especially after having received harsh criticism about the condition of the site two years earlier, was beginning to pay off. In 1924, another editorial appeared that praised the wonderful campground at the Rock. At a time when it was very expensive to travel and lodge a family during summer vacations, camping "made the cost of living while on the road almost as low as remaining at home, if expenses were carefully watched." And, Starved Rock State Park reportedly had "one of the most complete and up-to-date camping grounds to be found in the country." The site had large cooking ovens and the firewood was free. There was ample water for the "comfort building" that had "toilet accommodations for both sexes, with four shower baths....with hot and cold running water." And, an attendant was "delegated to look out for the wants of visitors, between four and five hundred of whom can be cared for at one time without crowding." The reported fame of the Starved Rock campground, according to one witness, was spreading. People from all over the country were enjoying the site. "See America first," it was proclaimed, "and in doing so don't overlook a bet by failing to plan to put in a few days at the Starved Rock State Park."

The accolades about the park kept coming. The Minonk Dispatch in 1926 reported that "Illinois' most beautiful spot is but an hour's ride from Minonk." How's that for resounding praise? The park is also "In touch with all hard roads." Besides the historic interest and natural beauty of the park, the site's campgrounds were again praised as being the model for all other campgrounds in the United States. Free camping, according to Col. Miller was "an experiment in human welfare" and an "adjunct to the good roads program of Governor Small."

In September 1926, the Chicago Tribune dispatched reporter James O'Donnell to Starved Rock State Park to checkout and report on the site. In an article about his visit, he noted that the park was both a playground and a schoolroom. O'Donnell reported that the park not only contains majestic and curious rock formations but it is also the site of two-hundred years of romantic and heroic history.

What about the condition of the park itself? Well, O'Donnell observed that the park was "cleanly kept," without signs that "belittle or disfigure" the natural beauty. The signs he saw were appropriately placed for which the "lawlessness and sluttishness of a considerable portion of the American people make necessary." These lawless ones, he pointed out included "paper strewers, flower pickers, diggers, promiscuous lunchers, firecracker shooters," and "inconsiderate parkers."

O'Donnell remarked that the hotel was "cheerful, if noisy." To him, it appeared to have been especially well run as it was kept under the watchful eye of a State inspector who looks after "affairs and hears complaints, if any." The hotel's concessionaire was Nicholas Spiros (who took over the lease following the January 1926 death of W.E. Crosier), whose employees were reportedly "agreeable young people" who were "studious to please." The hotel operated on the American plan, all posted rates included meals. Extra meal portions and extra service in the dining room were included in the price—there were no restrictions on the amount of food you could order. About this, O'Donnell wrote, "For your own sake get enough to eat—for humanity's sake do not waste." Great advice!

Not only did the hotel staff receive good reviews, so did the park employees. The park staff seemed to be "genuinely enamored" with the park's beauty. These reviews occurred before civil service testing and merit boards were established and overt politicization of state jobs sometimes occurred. With this in mind, O'Donnell asked Chicago Tribune political reporter Frank Butzow if he knew of any "political pull, graft, or scandal" pertaining to the management of Starved Rock State Park. Butzow replied that he had not heard anything to the park's "discredit," its operation was above board, or "clean," as he phrased it. This endorsement did not mean that politics did not play a role in the hiring process; it did. What it did mean was that it *appeared* that there was no *overt* corruption or the selling of jobs to the highest bidder (although there may have been instances of this).

No visit to Starved Rock State Park in 1926 would have been complete without a ride on the "Scenic Boat trip on the Illinois River." According to O'Donnell, it was "the best 35 cents worth I have had in many a day." Prior to the construction of the Starved Rock Lock and Dam, tour boats ferried site seers directly up the Illinois River from today's "sea wall," and landed at the mouth of Horseshoe Canyon (La Salle and Tonti Canyons were collectively known as Horseshoe Canyon) where passengers disembarked. Next, the site seers hiked the trail through the majestic white pines and within a few minutes gazed at La Salle Canyon (and waterfall if conditions permitted). Another ten-minute saunter would take them into Tonti Canyon.

The tour boat Pontiac on the Illinois River.

Another popular park attraction was the public swimming pool. Located due east from today's Visitor's Center, the pool was fed by an artesian well (nine-hundred fifty-nine feet deep) and was enclosed by a concrete wall. A mini-railroad train (originally from Lincoln Park Zoo in Chicago) ran around the outside perimeter of the pool. Inside the perimeter was a concrete island for sunbathers and a large waterslide. In addition, one could rent a board to ride a water chute from the top of the Devil's Nose (the sandstone bluff directly south of Starved Rock) to the pool below. For visitors who preferred to swim after dark the pool was equipped with floodlights.

The Starved Rock swimming pool.

In 1926 the hotel rates at the park were $4.50 per person for a room but rose to $6.00 per person if two or more people rented a room. Room rates were lower if they were rented by the week rather than by the day (meals were included in the price). The hotel had sixty-five guest rooms that could accommodate two-hundred-eighteen people. Round trip train rates between Chicago and Utica were $6.80. If you drove to the park, parking was free—the lot was touted as capable of holding over 15,000 cars. One park clerk at this time claimed that 15,640 cars were parked along the river one day and that "five-thousand visitors to the park on a Sunday is accounted a small day."

Two happy park visitors in 1934.

Starved Rock State Park was certainly growing in popularity, but then so were other notable state sites. According to one source, there were approximately 750,000 visitors to Starved Rock State Park in 1926. That same year, "More than a million enjoyed sights in Illinois public places during summer." The other state sites included Lincoln's monument (150,000), Lincolns' "Old Salem" park (75,000), Lincoln's homestead (40,000), Fort de Chartres (15,000), and Fort Massac (30,000). According to one report, "it is impossible to estimate the thousands who visited the Cahokia Mounds." The fledgling tourist industry was growing by leaps and bounds. The automobile, railways, and paved public roads contributed to this phenomenon which inadvertently spurred on growth in the restaurant, hotel/motel, camping, and other service- and tourist-related business.

3

Hiring a Park Custodian in the 1930's

As the park's renown grew, so did competition in the political world for employment at the famous site. With that said, let's take a look at the hiring process for the Site Custodian position at Starved Rock in 1929.

Louis Emmerson (a Republican) took office as Illinois governor in January 1929. With his new administration came the choice of who would fill a host of politically appointed State positions, such as the job of park custodian at Starved Rock. The park custodian at the time, James Williams, was no doubt concerned about his tenure as supervisor at the site. To this concern were letters written on his behalf. In July (remember that this is before the stock market crash), Frank J. Aimone of Cedar Point, Illinois (located about seven miles west of Starved Rock) wrote H.H. Cleaveland, then director of the Illinois Department of Public Works and Buildings, to retain Williams at the post. Amoine, a "staunch" Republican, described Williams as a "capable and efficient" custodian. Aimone requested that Cleaveland contact La Salle County officials including the County Clerk, Circuit Clerk, States Attorney, County Auditor, and even a County Judge, if he had concerns about Aimone's abilities or loyalty to the Republican party. Cleaveland replied that Aimone's letter will be filed "with others for reference when this matter is up for consideration." Cleaveland forwarded Aimone's recommendation up the political command chain to the Honorable Edmond Conerton (State Representative). Conerton wrote Cleaveland that "appointments are all being handled direct by the Governor." Cleaveland also wrote Governor Emmerson, advising that Williams' record is "quite satisfactory." Additional letters in support of Williams were written to John G. Boyle (State Superintendent of Illinois State Parks) by N.M. Mason, a high ranking school official of Oglesby, Illinois, and U.S. Congressman John T. Buckbee of Rockford.

Site Custodian Terrence Martin (left) and helpers sawing and splitting logs into firewood.

But in October, a new candidate for park custodian emerged, Walter Fox of Utica. It appeared that the tide of support for Williams was waning as Fox had the apparent endorsement of State Senator Reynolds of Utica, State Representatives Benson of Ottawa, and Governor Emmerson himself. On November 8, Cleaveland sent a memo to John Boyle (Cleaveland's park superintendent) to investigate Fox's "fitness for this position," and report back to him. Four days later Boyle notified his boss that Fox's son had been arrested "several times" for being "drunk and doing other things" and has been "cautioned several times since." Cleaveland then wrote the governor that "it would be a very great mistake to make this appointment" (of Fox). Cleaveland also wrote Harold Watson, State Administrative Auditor, that Fox was "thoroughly unqualified for the position." Apparent problems with Fox's background evidently disturbed the governor as he wrote to Cleaveland, "I wish to say that at your convenience I will discuss this matter with you." It appears that, since a suitable replacement for Williams was not available, the site custodian, temporarily anyway, retained his position.

By June 1930, reports of parties and drinking bouts concerning Williams were alleged (remember that this occurred during Prohibition, 1920-1933). Again, Cleaveland asked Boyle to determine if the allegations against Williams were true. Boyle later wrote back to his boss, "to my knowledge there has never been a booze or moonshine party at Jim William's house. I don't say that he has never taken a drink on State Property." The complaints against Custodian Williams reportedly came from a man named Robert Jessem, of whom Boyle had received "bad reports," and whom Custodian Williams had previously fired. It appears that Jessem may have been trying to smear the reputation of his former boss, to the benefit of Jack Fisher, a new candidate for the position of site custodian. Fisher was a "helper" employed by the State Highway Department whose work record was reported as "satisfactory." Fisher's boss, Michael Dunn, apparently did have some problem with Fisher's "aggressiveness," in that he believed that a qualified park custodian should be motivated and self-directed. If the custodian did not have these qualities, it was feared that "a great many things that should be done around the Park will go undone." A full year passed and the politicos were still unable to decide who would replace Custodian Williams.

By January of 1931, Cleaveland had concluded that "a change in the custodian position at Starved Rock Park" was due. Williams, evidently no longer curried favor with the powers in Springfield. Boyle received orders from Cleaveland to "interview Fisher yourself" to determine that he was the right person to replace Williams. We have no correspondence concerning Boyle's investigation of Fisher. What we do know is that Williams was still at the helm at the Rock as late as 1933, apparently by default.

Emmerson was a one-term governor of Illinois. Like many politicians who were in office when the stock market crashed and the Great Depression began, he was voted out. Emmerson was succeeded by Henry Horner (a Democrat) in 1933, who, like his predecessor, had the option—more likely the pleasure—of replacing all previous political appointees with people of his ilk. Accordingly, Cleaveland was no longer director, being replaced by Robert Kingery. And, a new candidate for park custodian emerged, Richard Costa of Utica. Costa was told to call the Governor's office to set up an interview for the position. It appears that for whatever reason, Costa did not fit the State template. However, a month later, George Malone a barber from La Salle, Illinois, became the new frontrunner in the race to become the park's custodian.

On April 7, 1933, over four years after the selection process began, Malone was officially chosen for the position. His appointment date was effective May 1. After reading the news of this change in management in the local newspapers (not from his employer), Williams tendered his resignation. Besides being provided a state house for a residence, of which he was required to furnish his own fuel, Malone was paid $100.00 per month. On Malone's letter of appointment was an important admonishment from Director Kingery that stated, "May I remind you that you will be the representative of the State of Illinois, and will meet many people in this State Park who will gain an impression of the administration and its management by your treatment of them. You must protect the Park and its property from vandalism and nuisance, but you must treat with your visitors always in a reasonable and fair manner." No clearer words could have been spoken to the person whose charge is the protection of the park and being the State's ambassador to the State's citizens.

One problem with the change in park management concerned William's resignation date and Malone's appointment date. Williams' resignation took effect on April 1 (even though Williams learned of the change on April 7) and Malone's appointment did not take effect until May 1. Concerning this, Director Kingery wrote Williams, "I am wondering if you would be so good as to remain in this position until April 30th?" In addition, Williams was instructed to inventory the tools and other items of value at the park before terminating employment with the state.

The park's night watchman was also replaced during this time. On July 2, 1932 Custodian Williams received a Western Union Telegraph from Cleaveland stating that Watchman Mason was to be replaced by William Pettigrew. The following year, Albert Schmidt was appointed night watchman of the park when the state administration changed from Republican to Democrat.

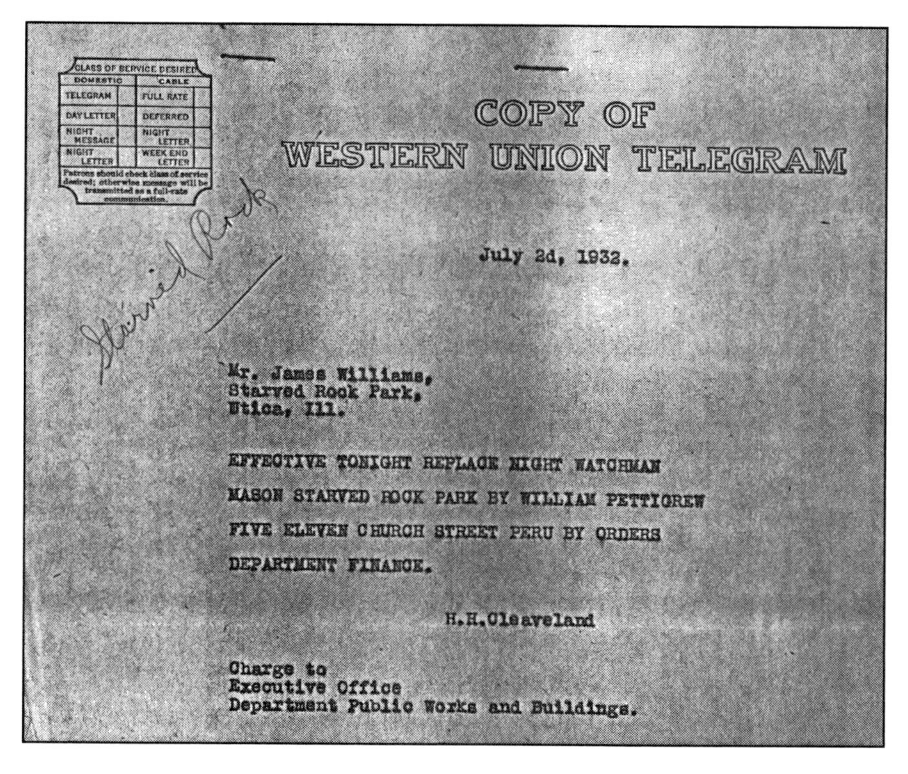

CLASS OF SERVICE DESIRED			
DOMESTIC		CABLE	
TELEGRAM		FULL RATE	
DAY LETTER		DEFERRED	
NIGHT MESSAGE		NIGHT LETTER	
NIGHT LETTER		WEEK END LETTER	

Patrons should check class of service desired; otherwise message will be transmitted as a full-rate communication.

COPY OF
WESTERN UNION TELEGRAM

Starved Rock

July 2d, 1932.

Mr. James Williams,
Starved Rock Park,
Utica, Ill.

EFFECTIVE TONIGHT REPLACE NIGHT WATCHMAN
MASON STARVED ROCK PARK BY WILLIAM PETTIGREW
FIVE ELEVEN CHURCH STREET PERU BY ORDERS
DEPARTMENT FINANCE.

H.H.Cleaveland

Charge to
Executive Office
Department Public Works and Buildings.

Copy of a western Union telegraph directing Williams to replace Night Watchman Mason dated July 2, 1932.

The park watchman position was an important one. His shift began at 8:00 pm and ended at 6:00 am. Specifically, he was to patrol the park campground and hotel concession area. Every night the campground's comfort station was to be hosed and cleaned. Campground quiet hours began at 10:00 pm and were to be enforced. Should campers arrive after quiet hours, the watchman was ordered to allow them to set up camp away from those already camping, "in order that the latter's sleep may not be disturbed." The later arrivals could obtain a camping permit the next day. As a sign of authority, the watchman was issued a Special Park Police badge. His salary in 1933 was $90.00 per month.

4

The 1930s and Great Depression Years

The Great Depression was a troubled time for many Americans. Unemployment soared, jobs were few and far between, and money was tight. But through it all Starved Rock State Park survived intact. Let's take a brief look at this challenging period of time to see what occurred at the famous park.

In 1932, Starved Rock State Park opened its doors to the public on Sunday, May 15. Just prior to the opening, park vendors and concessionaires and some local businesses went on a full media blitz to attract customers to their establishments. Full page ads in local newspapers advertised the musical entertainment and great fun that could be had at the park. Art Kassel and his "Kassels in the Air," straight from Chicago's Bismark Hotel, were coming to the hotel. Boat trips to Horseshoe Canyon with a view of the new Starved Rock lock and dam, and the new waterway lake (called the "Wide Waters" today) were advertised. La Salle-Peru Airways promoted "special passenger flights in our cabin plane" and "see Starved Rock from the air." After a spin or two on the dance floor, couples were directed to "meet your friends and make whoopee" at the Gateway, just north of Utica. It was the hip place to be. And it was "where the young folks get together." When the weather warmed, you could enjoy a dip in the Starved Rock pool and "get into the swim." If you planned to camp at the park, "Uncle Billy Bottomly" will be there to greet you.

The one and only Duke Ellington and his "Famous Orchestra" entertained guests at the Starved Rock Hotel on July 31. To get in the door to get a peek at the "Duke" cost thirty-five cents. But, if you chose to dance to his music, a fee of one dollar was required.

The Starved Rock Dance Pavilion.

The Illinois Department of Public Works and Buildings also did what it could to put a smiley face on the nation's economic woes. In 1932, the department a printed new brochure/booklet touting Starved Rock as the "Mecca of Romance and Indian Legendry." The booklet included a guide to the park's trail system, concessions, and campgrounds. The hotel, cafeteria, garage, swimming pool, dance hall, and even airplanes rides, along with tennis and golf were advertised in it. The park's canyons were called a "dreamland" for nature lovers. Visitors even learned a little about the sometimes forgotten French and Native American history of Illinois. But even though advertising the park concessions inadvertently commercialized the park, a practice often despised by people desirous of viewing the site's natural features, this was a time of great economic uncertainty and, as such, the State of Illinois made an effort to invigorate the economy. Therefore, a balance had to be struck between the commercial realities and natural attributes of the park—and the battle continues to this day.

Wooden retaining walls on the summit of Starved Rock, circa early 1930s.

Not only did the State of Illinois encourage people to visit the park, so did the Standard Oil Company. In 1932, the company issued a booklet entitled "Places to Go," a publication that was available at Standard Stations nationwide. The forty-five page work included the "high spots" of interest including five-hundred twenty-four "resorts" in thirteen Midwestern and Western states, including Starved Rock.

The effort to attract visitors worked. According to reports, "All attendance records for opening day at Starved Rock state park were shattered Sunday when more than 10,000 persons were at the park." There were also more than one-hundred guests for dinner at the Starved Rock Hotel that day. William Jasper and William Adams (dance hall co-concessionaires) reported that all dance pavilion records were broken when Art Kassel and his orchestra entertained the crowd. This attendance record reportedly exceeded the previous one that occurred two years earlier, when Guy Lombardo and his Royal Canadians played at the pavilion.

When George Malone became park custodian in the spring of 1933, he initiated a series of improvements to aid the public and increase safety. He bought a circular saw to cut branches, fallen trees and trees that were washed into the park during floods, into firewood to be utilized by campers. Malone also replaced the old trail markers (colored bands painted around the base of trees along the trails) with metal signs to direct hikers to places of interest in the park. Malone also repaired roads and washouts caused by heavy spring rains. Some of these safety improvements may have been in response to a thirteen-year-old Boy Scout who fell thirty feet into a canyon in May 1932. According to one report, the victim's companions (other Boy Scouts) administered first-aid on his broken wrist with crude splints and handkerchiefs and then walked him out of the canyon. After a doctor had examined and reset the scout's wrist, the boy was reportedly "ready for his evening meal."

Wildcat Canyon

During the same time, hotel concessionaire Nick Spiros redecorated the entire interior and exterior of the building. Later that summer, the park's dance pavilion hosted Jimmy Garrigan, "Direct from the Oriental Garden," on July 10 and Maurie Sherman and his College Inn Orchestra, "Favorites from the Aragon and Trianon" on the following Sunday.

Joseph Booton, Chief of Design, Division of Architecture and Engineering, Department of Public Works and Buildings, said that 1933 "was the depression's [Great Depression] low mark. Budgets were cut to the bone…." Accordingly, prices where lowered at park concessions to encourage business. Coffee was sold for five cents, as was "pop," ice cream cones, and cigars. With the end of Prohibition, beer was sold at the park. Hotel room rates were also reduced to as low as $3.00 per day, which included three meals per day. Parties of eight or more people could even see more reduced rates. To encourage the locals to patronize the park, advertisements were run in local newspapers that described the hotel as a "most delightful place to dine with your family or friends on Sunday or any evening of the week." Not only were hotel dinners "the best of foods," they were "correctly prepared, and served in surroundings you will enjoy and appreciate."

For a few miscreants in the 1930s, Starved Rock State Park was a place to steal from others. But Custodian Malone was up for the task. According to one account, Malone had received complaints that gas was being siphoned from parked cars during a dance at the park. Malone began "sleuthing" the area and caught the thieves red-handed. The gas thieves, five youths between the ages of seventeen and nineteen, were reportedly from Chicago. They had camped at the park for several days prior to their arrest. One of the thieves, Carl Haetzel, was reported to have been a "midget." Malone also added to his "laurels" by recovering an expensive watch that was accidentally left in the park and returning it to its owner. According to one report, a local boy named Wayne Donovan accidentally left his watch in the restroom while attending a dance at the pavilion. Malone was notified and after a two-week investigation, he learned that the watch had been "picked up in the restroom by a young farmer" who lived north of Utica. After learning that the watch's rightful owner had been found, the young farmer "readily turned it over" to Malone. For his good deed, the farmer was "rewarded" by Donovan's parents. Malone also established a "lost-and-found department," which was reported to have been "instrumental" in recovering and returning "many lost articles, a number of them worth considerable money, to their owners."

During this time, some people thought that a zoo at Starved Rock State Park would be a great idea. It was reported that Reverend Emanuel Crusius, a local clergyman, had urged the State of Illinois to "establish a zoo" at the site. Although the State probably never had any serious intentions of establishing a zoo at the park, we do know that they were working on a proposal to build a museum instead. The proposed museum would have been in conjunction with the Chicago Academy of Science, and would have featured mounts of past and present park wildlife. The museum never came to be either, but in its place the future Starved Rock Visitor's Center would be built.

Starved Rock State Park was also home base to Camp Starved Rock, Company 1609 of the Civilian Conservation Corps (CCCs). Their arrival at the park coincided with plans for a new hotel, today's Starved Rock Lodge. Although information about this period can be conflicting (depending on the source), we do know that by 1933, the idea for a new lodge had emerged. Reportedly, the Starved Rock Hotel, which in truth was more of a boarding house than fine living quarters, had seen its better days. Constructed in 1891, the old hotel was described as "a group of painted, unheated and inadequate buildings." But how to replace the old hotel during a Depression when "Budgets were cut to the bone" and "Funds were meager." The task seemed daunting.

Construction of the Starved Rock Lodge, May 10, 1938.

Keep in mind that, just because the State of Illinois thought that a new lodge was a good idea, it does not mean that everyone else thought it was. An editorial in the Ottawa Republican Times titled "Why a State Run Hotel?" (February 14, 1935) states that a rumor had been circulating that the state "contemplates the erection of a new hotel in Starved Rock state park." The editorialist complained that the state

SCHEDULE OF HOURS FOR CAMP GUARD
For Week Beginning Oct. 6, 1933 6:00 P.M.

Friday Oct. 6, 1933

6 P.M. - 10 P.M. Statt
10 P.M. - 2 A.M. Schumpp

Saturday Oct. 7, 1933

2 A.M. - 6 A.M. Schuelke
6 A.M. - 12 N. Statt
12 N. - 6 P.M. Schumpp
6 P.M. - 10 P.M. Schuelke
10 P.M. - 2 A.M. Statt

Sunday Oct. 8, 1933

2 A.M. - 6 A.M. Schumpp
6 A.M. - 12 N. Schuelke
12 N. - 6 P.M. Statt
6 P.M. - 10 P.M. Schumpp
10 P.M. - 2 A.M. Schuelke

Monday Oct. 9, 1933

2 A.M. - 6 A.M. Statt
6 A.M. - 12 N. Schumpp
12 N. - 6 P.M. Schuelke
6 P.M. - 10 P.M. Statt
10 P.M. - 2 A.M. Schumpp

Tuesday Oct. 10, 1933

2 A.M. - 6 A.M. Schuelke
6 A.M. - 12 N. Statt
12 N. - 6 P.M. Schumpp
6 P.M. - 10 P.M. Schuelke
10 P.M. - 2 A.M. Statt

Wednesday Oct. 11, 1933

2 A.M. - 6 A.M. Schumpp
6 A.M. - 12 N. Schuelke
12 N. - 6 P.M. Statt
6 P.M. - 10 P.M. Schumpp
10 P.M. - 2 A.M. Schuelke

Thursday Oct. 12, 1933

2 A.M. - 6 A.M. Statt
6 A.M. - 12 N. Schumpp
12 N. - 6 P.M. Schuelke
6 P.M. - 10 P.M. Statt
10 P.M. - 2 A.M. Schumpp

Friday Oct. 13, 1933

2 A.M. - 6 A.M. Schuelke
6 A.M. - 12 N. Statt

Guard on duty from 6 P.M. to 10 P.M. turn on Street lights at dusk and turn out tent lights at 9:30 P.M.

Guard on duty from 10 P.M. to 2 A.M. awaken foreman in charge for bed check at 11 P.M. After bed check turn out light on Company street.

Guard on duty from 2 A.M. to 6 A.M. awaken cook on duty and head K.P. at time notified. Raise flag at 5:45 A.M., wake bugler and foreman in charge. Turn out street lights.

Guards on duty from 12:00 Noon to 6 P.M. and 6 P.M. to 10 P.M. lower flag at retreat.

All guards awake during the day unroll tent flaps in case of rain.

Civilian Conservation Corps duty roster
for the week beginning October 6, 1933.

should not compete with "private firms and individuals." "There was a time" according to the writer "when a hotel in Starved Rock Park was next to a necessity." But that was before the "day of the automobile." Today, the writer pointed out, there are hotels in all communities that surround the park including Ottawa, La Salle, and Peru. Therefore, there is little demand for a hotel in the park. Though we might today think that this complaint was without merit, we see that some things never change. According to the editorial writer, "Illinois should not follow the lead of the national government which is now over its head in competition with private business." But despite this concern, a lodge was coming to the park.

According to Booton, the U.S. Government through the U.S. Army and Department of the Interior intended to establish a CCC camp at Starved Rock. But, with limited funds and tough economic times, the government had to get the biggest "bang for the buck." With this consideration, it was suggested that the CCCs construct a building with a dual purpose, the first to house the CCCs, and when they moved out, the structure could be modified and converted into the new lodge. The army liked the idea and immediately made arrangements for plans to be drawn up for the project. In the meantime, barracks were built at the park to house the CCCs and work began on trail construction, bridge building, and the construction of shelters. To insure that the government was not competing with local privately owned construction contractors, the CCCs were only allowed to erect buildings that cost less than $5,000.00.

In 1934, park authorities received the plans for the project and they purchased the necessary materials. The CCCs began their work by laying a gravel floor and then building a shelter on top of it. This structure, according to Booton, stood as a picnic and barbeque spot for the next two years.

The following year, state and federal governments appropriated $60,000.00 for the CCC lodge project (federal grant of $45,733.51 and state contribution of $14,266.49). During this time, twelve fashionable log cabins were built on the future site of the lodge. These structures were built in two even rows of six, as it was hoped that a corridor could be built connecting the cabins and a second story built above. The idea, however, was cost prohibitive—more rooms could be built for less money in an entirely hotel new wing if it was built by simple construction. In 1936, the CCCs enclosed their shelter and constructed the lodge's dining room and kitchen wing, complete with water, lights, and heat. While the CCCs waited for the plans for the new lodge to arrive and for the purchase of construction materials, they busied themselves with other park projects (e.g. trail work and bridge building). In 1938 construction of the lodge's room wing was to commence. But first, the twelve cabins on the lodge site had to be disassembled and moved to a new location. This was done by the CCCs and today visitors can see the old cabins located a short distance south of Fox Canyon (a few are located west of the lodge swimming pool). After the construction contracts were awarded and materials were delivered, construction of the present Starved Rock Lodge began. In January 1939, the Starved Rock Lodge was open for business.

The newly constructed Starved Rock Lodge dining hall.

The CCCs also completed other work around the new lodge. They cleared trees, built the lodge road, built the lodge parking lot, erected signs, and landscaped around the new buildings. The CCCs laid the new stone steps that lead to the summit of Starved Rock. On top, they

One of the cabins that occupied the future site of today's Starved Rock Lodge that was relocated

also built a stone retaining wall around the summit's outer perimeter and filled the inside of the wall with dirt to protect the site from erosion. Still visible today, the wall and stairs were made from "Fond du Lac Weathered Stone" purchased from Ecco Material Corporation in Chicago. The federal government chipped in $331.95 for the project while the state paid the lion's share of the cost, $2015.00. Although there were actually three CCC companies assigned to Starved Rock State Park during this time, only one of them called the site home (the 1609th).

When the new Starved Rock Lodge was open for business, the old Starved Rock Hotel was closed. Although the old hotel sat vacant for a little over a year, it was eventually demolished and removed. The site where it once stood is directly adjacent to Starved Rock, on the terrace called "the Hotel Plaza."

Stone retaining walls on the summit of Starved Rock
that were constructed by the CCCs

A hallway in the new Starved Rock Lodge
photographed on January 11, 1939

By 1938, Starved Rock State Park had a "Park Naturalist" in its employ, Dr. Donald Ries. On September 11, 1938, Ries hosted the park's annual "nature tour," the program of events is detailed as follows:

Morning Program

Under direction of John B. Gilmour, Federal Recreation Service

9:30 am: Flag raising ceremony. La Salle Boy Scouts Drum and Bugle Corps. On top of Starved Rock.
10:00 am: Field Mass. Conducted by Rev. George M. Link, Pere Marquette State Park. North lawn of hotel.
11:00 am: Non-denominational service. Conducted by Rev. M.A. Darroch, Utica Baptist Church, Utica, IL. North lawn of hotel.

Afternoon Program

Under direction of Donald T. Ries, Park Naturalist

1:30 pm: General discussion of park. Dr. Donald T. Ries, north lawn of hotel. From this point groups will be taken to the other speakers listed below.

History: Rev. G.M. Link, State Naturalist, Pere Marquette. On top of Starved Rock.
Geology: Dr. George Ekblaw, Illinois State Geological Survey. Top of Lover's Leap
Botany: Dr. George Fuller, University of Chicago, near top of Jacob's Ladder.
Birds: Mr. George Hawkins. Illinois State Natural History Survey. South of Turtle Rock.
Mammals: Dr. Carl O. Mohr, Illinois State Natural History Survey. Near entrance of French Canyon.
Astronomy: Rev. George Link and Dr. Ries. On lawn north of hotel. Weather Permitting.

The Park Naturalist was the forerunner of the Park Interpreter and today's Program Coordinator, a position whose work was conducted a bit more formally than it is today.

In addition to the improvements and renovations that were occurring at Starved Rock State Park in the 1930s, another large government project was in progress. This was the construction of the Starved Rock Lock and Dam. Originally started by the state in the late 1920s, the project ran out of funds during the Great Depression. The partially completed dam was finished by the United States Government and became operational in 1933. The dam was built to open the Upper Illinois River to commercial navigation between Chicago and the Mississippi Valley.

A view of Plum Island taken from the summit of Starved Rock in 1932.

The Upper Illinois River, between its source at the confluence of the Des Plaines and Kankakee Rivers to its merger with the ancient Mississippi River at the "Big Bend," is a relatively new body of water—having been formed about 13,000-14,000 years ago by rushing glacial melt water (Kankakee Torrent). The torrent exposed rocks that formed a long series of rapids in front of Starved Rock and at today's Marseilles. These rapids halted upstream commercial navigation of the river at a point just above La Salle, Illinois. To by-pass the rapids and open commerce between Chicago and the Mississippi Valley (e.g. New Orleans, St. Louis), the Illinois and Michigan Canal was dug (previously, the Erie Canal was dug through New York State and connected the New York markets with the Great Lakes). With the major water routes of the region connected, the stockade, fur trade post, and frontier settlement of Chicago grew exponentially, ultimately finding itself at the center of Midwestern commerce (timber and iron ore from the north, grain and limestone from the heartland, and coal from the south).

A view of the Starved Rock locks.

But, even though the new Starved Rock Lock and Dam was a boon to commerce, it did cause a few minor problems for the park. The river level above the dam rose about ten feet which inadvertently caused erosion to the south shoreline. Water levels also flooded the islands above the dam, some of which were owned by the State of Illinois. Tour boats could no longer navigate directly upstream from the park's Lower Area Seawall to Horseshoe Canyon. They now had to cross the river and moor near the locks on the north side. Passengers then had to disembark, walk to the east side of the dam, and board a second passenger boat, which carried them to Horseshoe Canyon.

Future years would see fewer dramatic changes at the park. Nevertheless, the park would still experience growth and quite a few interesting moments.

5

The Modern Park Era

The old hotel was gone; the lodge and dining hall was up and running; park concessions were selling food, souvenirs, and clothes; new stairways, bridges, and walkways had been built; and paved roads facilitated vehicular traffic. To maintain the park, the state hired several new employees, both part-time and full-time. Park employees in 1943 earned sixty cents per hour, a fifteen-cent- per-hour increase over 1942's wages. But at the same time, the park's payroll was reduced by $464.25 (in a total payroll budget of $2,150.80) from the previous year. In addition, spring flooding damaged the park's Lower Area and caused "considerable damage" to the parking lot, campground, and picnic area. That year it required 1,200 man hours of labor to clean up the mess left by the spring floods. With a smaller budget and more work to do, the park's finances were again stretched to the limit.

Not only could visitors explore the wonders of Starved Rock State Park; they now had an adjacent state park to discover. In 1942, the Blow estate donated 176 acres of land to the State of Illinois, which in turn made the new acquisition a satellite park of Starved Rock. Prior to state ownership the property had been a private park known as the Deer Park Nature Area. The new site, located about a mile south of Starved Rock State Park, was renamed Matthiessen State Park in honor of local industrialist, entrepreneur, and philanthropist Frederick William

Matthiessen. While Starved Rock Park proper is known for its eighteen canyons and many hiking trails, the new Matthiessen addition consists of one very large canyon with hiking trails interspersed along its course.

Streator postal service at the Deer Park Nature Area in 1910, today's Matthiessen State Park

The Starved Rock Lodge was built on the site of the original park campgrounds. A replacement site, therefore, had to be found. Park officials determined that the new camp should be located in the Lower Area, along the Illinois River, adjacent to today's boat ramp (an area commonly known today as the "Beer Gardens"). Although the new area was large enough to hold hundreds of campers, it had one major disadvantage, it was located along the river and subject to flooding (floods happen as many as seven times per year). But that didn't bother the United States Army, which sent an engineering detachment to train at the park during World War II. The men of the detachment perfected their skill of building pontoon bridges that would be used in the coming invasion of Europe. Army tents were set up in military order along the river next to jeeps, pontoons, and other equipment. The army also set up a canteen on the east side of the street, mid-block, in downtown Utica to serve the soldiers.

So what would a visitor do at Starved Rock State Park in the 1940s? Of course, many of the same things we would do today such as having a picnic, going on a hike, or taking a boat ride. But at that time, dances were still popular at the park's dance pavilion on Thursdays and Sunday nights, swimmers and sunbathers relaxed at the pool, and Park Naturalists gave "daily" guided hikes, except on Tuesdays.

La Salle Canyon

Visitors could also go horseback riding at a private stable located near today's west park entrance. For cosmetic purposes, the stable's horses were often brushed and curried by local kids every spring, after the animals returned from their winter sojourn west of the park. These same horses were sometimes hitched to a carriage and driven to Utica to pick up visitors at the train depot, who would then be transported to the lodge. This system of communication was made possible through wireless technology wherein engineers would contact the lodge to know if a passenger(s) needed to be dropped off or picked up at the Utica train station.

Visitors could take an airplane ride that flew from a landing strip on Plum Island. To get to the island, visitors rode the ferry boat across the south channel of the river, disembarked, and then boarded a small passenger plane. There was also a small pavilion used for dances that were sometimes held on the island. During the Fourth of July weekend, park visitors could also watch the fireworks that were shot from the island.

The Starved Rock Lodge had a great restaurant. However, to some local folks, the establishment seemed to cater to wealthier locals and tourists from Chicago—it was a bit too expensive to take the family there for dinner. The only time that many local folks ate at the lodge was when a family member received his or her First Holy Communion, graduated from high school, or completed some important "rite of passage." The price of meals at the lodge was the same, regardless of what the customer ordered. In other words, all breakfasts were the same price, as were all lunches, and all suppers.

Dinner guests at the Starved Rock Lodge in 1939.

During the 1940s and early 1950s, local residents came to the park sometimes every day, especially during the hot summer months. Since few homes had air conditioning during this time, the park was a great place to walk along the river, skip stones, and cool off. The narrow park roads with ridiculously low speed limits were ideal for car loads of kids with their windows rolled down to beat the heat. One local resident said that one of the coolest places in the park (temperature-wise) was at the west end of the park's west entrance road, where the road is closest to the cool sandstone cliffs.

Local groups like the Utica Campfire Girls were often weekend visitors at the park. On occasional Sundays, the Campfire Girls would pack a lunch, cross the old river swing bridge, and hike the park, sometimes venturing as far east as Horseshoe Canyon. After they reached their destination and ate their lunch, the girls would retrace their steps and hike back home to Utica.

Bridge at Horseshoe Canyon

A different form of entertainment took place just east of today's Visitor's Center. There, during the summer, a stage was usually erected for local political gatherings, musical entertainment, talent shows, and other kinds of performances. Remember that not every home in the Illinois Valley had a television set at that time. Getting out of the house to see what was happening at the outdoor stage or watch who was performing there was a fun thing to do.

Park visitors could also experience some of the Native American history of the Starved Rock area. Sam Sine, also known as "Chief Walks-With-The-Wind," a Native American of the Winnebago tribe, entertained visitors at the park and lodge for decades. He gave talks, operated a small archery range, and hosted pow-wows at "Indianland," a site atop a sandstone bluff near the west entrance of the park. He was also involved in many other local public activities. Visitors remember him dressed in full "tribal regalia," a picture of which is proudly displayed at today's Starved Rock Visitor's Center. Another Native American celebrity of sorts was a man known to the locals as "Indian Frank." Frank Hart, a Seneca Indian, operated a small concession at the junction of the trail leading to French Canyon and Lover's Leap. There he did beadwork and operated a "wishing well" located directly adjacent to his "tee-pee."

In 1953, a pony ride concession was operated in today's Lower Area, directly west of today's visitor's center and on the north side of the main park road. The ponies were tethered to a post with a long lead and were walked in circles around it, led by local teenage employees. Twenty-five cents could buy the rider ten laps around the post.

Yet, during the 1950s, the powers in Springfield determined that admission should be charged at all state parks that were at least one-hundred acres in size. The only exception to this rule was Lincoln's New Salem State Park near Petersburg, Illinois, about twenty miles northwest of Springfield. The implementation of this program had the immediate effect of stopping local residents from visiting the park. Why should they pay to go to a place that they have visited for free all of their lives? Although the park was a place of fun and many fond memories, it seemed to them that, again, the site was catering to Chicago tourists who spent money at the privately run concessions.

As a consequence of the admission fees, local entrepreneurs established small businesses just outside of the park boundaries. Along the south entrance road of the park, the Arrowhead Motel lodged park visitors in relative comfort. Across the road was Harbeck's root beer stand, which sold cold soft drinks from the 1950's through the 1970s. Mother Goose Gardens, located at the old south entrance road at Illinois Route 71, was a place where costumed fairy tale characters greeted children. It was also where kids rode a miniature train that wove through the park and where they enjoyed amusement rides.

Old south entrance to Starved Rock State Park

Park visitors from the late 1940s through the 1960s were extremely fortunate to have had experienced a guided hike or heard a presentation by Robert T. Burns. Burns taught at Ottawa Township High School, in Ottawa, Illinois and also worked as a part-time nature guide at the park. He also wrote books (*Partners in Progress; Pioneers, Pow Wows and*

Prairie Playgrounds) pamphlets and booklets *(Guideline: Starved Rock; Link to the Past),* and articles about La Salle County and Starved Rock in *Outdoor Illinois.* Loved by many, Burns intimately knew the history and geology of the region, as well as much about its unique fauna and flora. He was said to have "roamed 6,000 miles" through Starved Rock State Park while leading hikes. The park was very fortunate to have had this great teacher as an ambassador in its employ for the edification of its visitors.

With newer and better roads having been built and the consequent additional influx of park visitors, combined with increased truck traffic to local quarries and grain elevators, the old Utica swing bridge that spanned the Illinois River became obsolete. Construction of a new bridge and the massive job of filling in a large ravine, building a berm, and laying a roadway on top of it got underway in the early 1960s. In addition, with the construction of the berm on Illinois Route 178, the west entrance road of the park had to be raised many feet to connect to the highway. Thousands of yards of earth and tons of stone were required for the project. When it was completed, the new state highway ran south of the Illinois River and up the south bluff. The new road covered the old horse rental and, unfortunately, a Woodland period Indian mound known as the Box Elder Mound. The new bridge and new section of highway was open for vehicular traffic in 1962. Remnants of the old roadway can still be seen just below and east of Route 178, and north of the west park entrance road.

In 1967, the park gained additional property when five-hundred and two acres of land were donated to the Department of Conservation and the Illinois Nature Preserves Commission (In 1951 the Division of Parks and Memorials was transferred to the Illinois Department of Conservation). Much of the property is located today between the Illinois River and Illinois Route 71 (west of Illinois Route 178), and extends nearly all of the way to the Vermilion River. The State was required to protect the park from "encroachment" and to ensure that the land would be properly managed as an "undeveloped wilderness." Although the site was difficult to access, it was hoped that "primitive trails" would eventually be provided for public access.

In 1973, the boat ride concessions in large vessels such as the Starved Rock Queen ended. In response to the increasing number of bald eagles that began wintering in front of the Starved Rock dam, the plane rides that left Plum Island ended in 1975. That same year the campground along the river was closed and moved to today's location, on East 950th Road, south of Illinois Route 71.

A tour boat takes park visitors on a cruise of the Illinois River in front of Starved Rock

Changes in park personnel and changes in their respective duties also occurred during this time. In 1976, Starved Rock Site Superintendent Jack Querciagrossa transferred to Matthiessen State Park and was replaced by Jon Blume, site manager of Lincoln's New Salem State Park. Under Blume, park personnel who had been assigned to maintenance duties at the lodge, a state owned building, were reassigned to duties that pertained to the rest of the park. The lodge concessionaire was now responsible for all maintenance work required at the lodge.

Important trail projects designed to protect the park from over use and for public safety were also initiated. In 1981, a wooden walkway was constructed around the perimeter of Starved Rock's summit to protect the site from erosion. In 1982, wooden overlooks were built on the Lover's Leap, Eagle Cliff, Owl Canyon, and Hennepin Canyon bluffs and Beehive Rock.

Construction of the new wooden walkway on the summit of Starved Rock, 1981.

In 1988-1989 the State of Illinois expanded, renovated and made improvements to the Starved Rock Lodge. Additional hotel rooms were added, as were a swimming pool and new lounge. To facilitate the expected increase of vehicles, a new parking lot had to be built. Unfortunately, the idea of cutting several acres of mature timber did not go over well with some nature lovers. Editorials in local papers lamented the loss of the trees. But the outcry did nothing to halt construction of the parking lot, and today few people if any even remember the contention that occurred at the time.

A photograph of various CCC Company #1609 personnel presenting a CCC plaque to Illinois Governor Thompson at the time of the grand re-opening of the Starved Rock Lodge in May 1988.

With the construction of the new lodge additions and parking lot, the old Visitor's Center had to be moved or demolished. The latter course was taken, as the dilapidated building stood in the way of progress. To replace the old Visitor's Center, a single-wide house trailer was placed below the bluff in the Lower Area, directly west of the west entrance of today's Visitor's Center. The single-wide structure was replaced a few years later with a double-wide trailer, which stood at the site until October 2002.

During the summer of 1995, the same year that the Illinois Department of Conservation became the Illinois Department of

Natural Resources, heavy rains doused North Central Illinois. The Fox and Illinois rivers swelled beyond their banks, homes were flooded and property was damaged. As a result of the deluge, standing water and mud on several of the park's upper trails made hiking difficult if not messy. Conditions on the Campanula trail in particular caused hikers to walk on the edge of the trail which inadvertently caused it to widen with every new footstep. Something had to be done to protect the fragile flora that was being trampled by hikers. Park staff devised a plan to construct a wooden walkway along the trial that would extend from French Canyon Creek, to within a few hundred feet from Wildcat Canyon. Work commenced and when the walkway was completed, hikers (and people with small children in strollers, etc.) had easier, cleaner, and more user-friendly access to the south rim of the park. The park's plant life, some of which is rare in Illinois, was also protected.

One of the park's temporary visitor's centers before the new building was completed in 2002.

A Bluebell, a common spring wildflower at Starved Rock State Park.

Between 1997 and 1999, a three phase project to protect the park's fragile eco system and enhance public safety was completed. The first phase of the project was the construction of a wooden staircase (commonly called Jacob's Ladder) from lower French Canyon Creek to the top of the east summit of the Lover's Leap Bluff. On top of the bluff, a wooden walkway was built to guide visitors to the Lover's Leap overlook. The second phase of the project connected the Lover's Leap overlook with the Eagle Cliff overlook via a continuation of the wooden walkway. The third and final phase of the project was shoreline stabilization, to protect the park's shoreline from erosion caused by the strong Illinois River current. During this phase, "tri-lock," three-way interlocking concrete stars were laid along the river shoreline between the park's "sea wall" and the recently renovated boat ramps. Above the Starved Rock Dam, rip-rap boulders were placed along the south shoreline and were then covered with cement. Also during this time, the old and rapidly deteriorating sea wall was removed and a new wall complete with railings was built.

The stairway known as Jacob's Ladder.

Starved Rock State Park was also a site where state and federal jobs programs were initiated. Programs such as the Youth Conservation Corps (the later Illinois Conservation Corps) gave teenagers and young adults an opportunity to work at the park and to learn new skills. These workers did many things—they picked up garbage, maintained and serviced park equipment, and built fences. The Green Thumb program was designed to give older Americans seasonal employment opportunities with the state. Their duties included, among many things, mowing grass (and there is a lot of this!), planting trees, and painting and maintaining park benches, picnic tables, and signs. During the summer, the park offered part-time employment in the form of "conservation workers," employees who assist park staff with a variety of duties. Other programs included the Comprehensive Educational Training Act (CETA), a federal program that provided state and local agencies block grants to employ economically disadvantaged, unemployed, or under employed people. The Business Employment Skills Team (BEST) a private organization in La Salle, Bureau, Putnam, and Lee counties that helps people find everything from scholarships to employment, partnered with Starved Rock park staff.

Between 1981 and 2005 attendance at the park increased from 1,255,298 to 2,012,063, with 2004 the high point at 2,122,422. Events such as the Turn of the Century, Montreal Canoe Weekend, Winter Wilderness Weekend, and many others drew large crowds to the park. More and more people were coming to the park.

A helicopter bringing wooden decking to workers building the new walkways at the park.

During the autumn of 2000, Starved Rock State Park officially held its first whitetail deer hunting season. Hunting pressure on private property outside of the park drove large herds of deer onto park property. The ever increasing size of the herd became a nuisance. Car/motorcycle-deer accidents around the park were numerous, hungry deer decimated the crops of local farmers, and rare plants, some of them endangered species, were eaten. Some parts of the park had deer populations of over 180 deer per square mile, an unsustainable number of creatures. The new deer season at the park effectively thinned the deer herd to a manageable level that caused less damage to crops, park flora, and passing motorists. It also gave hunting opportunities to Illinois hunters who had no place to hunt.

A *voyageur's* canoe paddled by park visitors during the Montreal Canoe Weekend.

When the deer hunting program was initiated, additional employees to operate the check station, assist handicap hunters, and open and close parts of the site were not part of the package. In 1976, Starved Rock employed twenty-four full-time maintenance employees, rangers, and other help while Matthiessen State Park employed four. Assisting those workers were summer conservation workers and people employed in the previously mentioned seasonal federal and state programs. By 1990 there were fifteen Starved Rock and two Matthiessen employees and in 2009 there were thirteen employees at Starved Rock and none at Matthiessen. It should be noted that three of the Starved Rock thirteen employees are security personnel and one is an office assistant, none of whom perform park maintenance or upkeep. With more things to do and less staff to do them, park employees worked harder than ever to serve the public. Unfortunately, shifting employees to do different duties left other duties undone. Between mid-November and early March, when park employees usually spent much time repairing trails, cutting trees, and performing miscellaneous outdoor maintenance work, they were now facilitating hunting programs. In 1996, for example, park staff spent ninety-seven days on the trails. In 1997, they spent one-hundred six days doing trail work. In 1998 they worked ninety-three days on the trails. By way of contrast, they spent only thirty-nine days on the trails in 2000, seventy-six days in 2001, and only twenty-three days in 2002. But even though these statistics may be cause for concern to some people, one thing is for certain: in the hearts of every member of the Starved Rock State Park staff is a reflection of Public Works and Buildings Director Robert Kingery's admonition to Park Custodian George Malone in 1933, "May I remind you that you will be the representative of the State of Illinois, and will meet many people in this State Park who will gain an impression of the administration and its management by your treatment of them. You must protect the Park and its property from vandalism and nuisance, but you must treat with your visitors always in a reasonable and fair manner."

After many years of delay, construction of the long anticipated park Visitor's Center began in 2001. After suffering through years of representing the park in wooden shacks and hand-me-down mobile homes, the site would now have a building that reflected the park at its best. But before construction could begin, the old park concession stands, remnants of days of old that once stood adjacent to the temporary Visitor's Centers, had to be demolished. The old Works Progress Administration (WPA) building next to concessions also had to go. The site of the new building also had to be surveyed by archaeologists to make sure that the new structure was not built on an archaeological site. Work on the new Visitor's Center eventually began, and in October of 2002, its doors were open to the public.

With the Visitor's Center open, the park staff had even more work to do, with still fewer people to do it with. An information desk needed to be manned to answer questions, complaints, and calls for service. The building needed to be cleaned as hundreds, sometimes thousands of visitors passed through its doors daily. Someone also had to deal with fish tanks, burned out light bulbs, displays, plugged toilets, broken water fountains, and a myriad of other mishaps. Fortunately, help was at hand. In 1992 a not-for-profit foundation was formed to "facilitate the Visitor's Center programs that include education, conservation, and recreation." Members of the Starved Rock Historical and Education Foundation volunteer their time to make sure that the Visitor's Center remains open and keeps running. The foundation mans the information desk, conducts guided hikes, provides educational programs for children and adults, and hosts annual events. The foundation also operates the Le Rocher Bookstore, proceeds from which STAY AT THE PARK. Revenues earned at the bookstore purchase equipment for the park that would otherwise be unavailable to staff. In addition, park benches, birding areas, binoculars for public use, computers, and host of other items were purchased by the foundation and donated to the park.

Today's Starved Rock Visitor's Center.

6
Park Legends

No historical survey of Starved Rock State Park would be complete without a brief look at a few notable park legends. Even though this subject may be a bit beyond the official scope of this book, I think it is important to devote a page or two to explain what is known about them.

Many park visitors ask about the Legend of Lover's Leap. What happened to give the site its name? To begin, there are several different versions of the legend—none of which give an account of an actual historical event. One of these was published in 1915 and is titled "Lolomi of the Illinois: A Legend of Lovers Leap." In this story an Indian maiden who was betrothed to Uncas, son of Chief Chassagoac, was shunned by her fiancé. When Lolomi heard that Uncas was married to another woman, she ran to throw herself from the Lover's Leap bluff and into the river below. The Indian messenger who brought her the news about Uncas grabbed her, brought her back to her village, and delivered her to her father, Chief Blackhawk. Her father placed her under a continuous watch, but she escaped and threw herself from the Lover's Leap cliff. Barely alive, she was pulled from the water. The last word she uttered was "Uncas."

Another version of this story also dates to 1915. In this tale, Wauwatosa, (the "Wild Rose of the Prairie") learned that her fiancé married a different Indian maiden. With her soul and spirit having been cut to the quick, she climbed the famous Lover's Leap bluff, sang her tribe's death song, and then hurled herself from its heights. They say that her soul "at last found rest."

A photograph of the Lover's Leap/Eagle Cliff bluff many years before the construction of the Starved Rock Dam.

Neither of these tales has any truth to it. They are different versions of old legends that are told all over America and other countries. Similar Lover's Leaps, and the accompanying myth, are found near South Lake Tahoe, California; in Fayette County, West Virginia; in Kimble County, Texas; near Chattanooga, Tennessee; in Madison County, North Carolina; in Western Maryland; and near New Milford, Connecticut. There are also Lover's Leaps in Jamaica, Ireland, and Guam (the latter site has a statue of the lovers). It is interesting to note that early maps of Starved Rock State Park (pre-1924) call today's Lover's Leap "Maiden Rock," a reference to the site of the mythical event.

Another legend concerns French trader and explorer Henri Tonti (it is not "de Tonti"), La Salle's second in command. According to the legend, Tonti was falsely accused of violating his royal trade contract, and he was ordered to hand-over his trade operations to an undeserving Frenchman. Tonti left Starved Rock and lived in the French settlements on the Gulf of Mexico. He returned to the Rock many years later, a tired broken old man. When the local Indians learned that their old friend Tonti had returned to the area, they rushed to see him. Unfortunately, Tonti soon died and his body was reportedly buried at the west end of the famous Rock.

In reality, Tonti and his trading partner La Forest were accused of violating restrictions on the Illinois trade, and Tonti left today's Illinois permanently in 1702. However, he died of yellow fever at today's Mobile Bay, Alabama, in 1704. Tonti is buried somewhere near the site of the old French fort there. He never returned to the fort at Starved Rock (The fort at Starved Rock had been abandoned in 1691). Be that as it may, this has not deterred others from their insistence that Tonti did return to the Rock before he died. In fact, in 1891, the Ottawa Free Trader reported that "The excavations at Starved Rock..... have resulted in finding the grave and remains of the famous French commander Tonti." Reportedly, the newly discovered grave had been prepared with "much care." Buried with the body were bits of richly inlaid armor. But the most telling clue to the identity of the human remains was an artificial bronze hand that was allegedly found in the grave (Tonti reportedly had an artificial hand that replaced a real one that was shot off in Sicily). The hand was reported to have had "steel joints" as it "must have bee [been] of intricate mechanism." In recent years I have personally encountered local residents who maintain that Tonti's grave, complete with an iron hand, was found at the park. The same article that relayed the news of this find also contains a correction that reads "The story of the finding of the grave and iron hand of Tonti at Starved Rock, so pompously telegraphed to a Chicago paper, turns out to have been a genuine joke. The people at the Rock know nothing about any such find and laugh at the story as a good joke." Again, this time in 1914, another skeleton was unearthed at the park while workers were digging a sewer line. And again, it was reported in the newspaper that some folks believed that the remains belonged to Tonti. More than likely, the skeletal remains were of a Native American who lived at today's Starved Rock State Park many years ago.

In another legend, Tonti buried a hoard of gold on or somewhere around the Rock. This legend was popularized in the 1870s by Nehemiah Matson author of *The French and Indians of the Illinois River* (1874). According to Matson, Tonti buried his gold before he left Illinois, planning to retrieve it later. He never did. News of the gold on the Rock consequently spurred local resident to dig the site's summit to find the lost riches. The truth is, Tonti never had gold or riches. In fact, he was probably deep in debt when he left Illinois in 1702. About the Western fur trade he once wrote, "There is no more trade since it has been forbidden by the court [French king]. All the voyages I made for the success of this country have ruined me."

In the 1920s, a pamphlet that sold for ten cents reported that gold had been buried on the summit of the Rock. This gold, however, was not Tonti's. It belonged to "Chassagear," a great Illinois chief who allegedly died in 1714. The pamphlet said that "a large quantity of gold images, crosses and crucifixes" had been placed in his grave. Although the same account states that Chassagear's burial mound can still be seen, it had been reportedly robbed by a Potawatomi chief named Watas some years after the internment.

Another account of buried treasure at the Rock comes from the La Salle Daily Tribune, in an article printed in 1914. In the story, a man "who claimed La Salle [Illinois] as his home told a few interested friends" that there was treasure buried at the park. The man allegedly corroborated his story by producing an old treasure map. The treasure was allegedly buried at the Rock by a band of Indians who "in fear of attack by a hostile tribe, either fled from the vicinity or were starved to death when surrounded on the lofty summit."

A pseudo-legend of sorts made its debut in the 1930s when two local men reportedly unearthed French and Native items on private property near the park at a site known today as the Newell Site or Newell Fort.

The discovery prompted some people to declare that the items were evidence of La Salle's Fort Saint Louis, a place generally assumed by historians to have been on top of Starved Rock. Letters were written to the Chicago Tribune's Voice of the People decrying that the state had assumed wrongly that the fort was on Starved Rock. In response, Robert Kingery, Acting Director of the Illinois Department of Public Works and Buildings, wrote to the Tribune, assuring them that volumes of historical documents, many written by La Salle himself, prove that the fort was indeed on Starved Rock. Some of the artifacts uncovered by the men are on display at the Starved Rock Visitors Center.

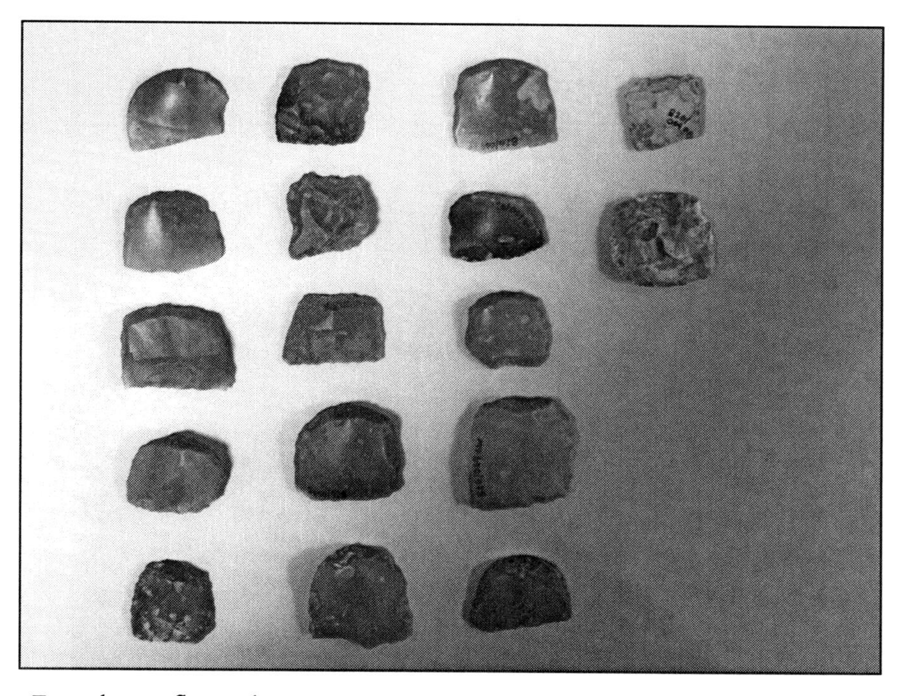

French gunflints that were reportedly found by two local men in the 1930s on display at the Starved Rock Visitor's Center.

A photograph taken at the south entrance of Starved Rock State Park in the early 1930s that advertises the alleged site of Fort Saint Louis.

7

Today

This year, 2011, Starved Rock State Park celebrates the completion of its first century as a public park. The park is still a wonderful place to visit. The park's canyons are still beautiful, the park's diverse and lush vegetation is as healthy as ever, and the park's wildlife is still abundant. The park's trails are well marked with signs, are protected with wooden walkways, and have been altered and sometimes rerouted for public safety. In addition, the lodge hosts guests from all over the world, the campground is still the model that other campgrounds emulate, and boat rides still take passengers around Plum Island on an excursion on the historic and beautiful Illinois River. Another interesting fact is that in 2009, Starved Rock State Park was voted one of the Seven Wonders of Illinois by the citizens of Illinois.

A stop at the Starved Rock Visitor's Center is a must for everyone. There you can watch videos that explain what to see at the park, that relate the French Native American history of the area, and that discuss the role of the CCCs at the park. Among many things, the Visitor's Center has an information desk, numerous displays, and a great little bookstore.

A view of the Lover's Leap bluff and the Starved Rock dam during the winter

Please come and visit us at the park and enjoy Illinois at its best. You will never forget that day you spent there!

Appendix A

The following is a synopsis of some archaeological work that has been performed on the summit of Starved Rock.

Before mentioning the archaeological work performed at the park, it must be noted that it is illegal to look for, take, or displace any artifact on any state property. The Illinois Conservation Police strictly enforce the provisions of the Archaeological and Paleontological Resource Protection Act and the Human Grave Protection Act at Starved Rock and all state parks. Violations of these acts include fines of up to $10,000.00 and/or incarceration of up to three years.

- **1947**: Exploratory excavations on the summit of the Rock under the supervision of Kenneth G. Orr of the University of Chicago and John C. McGregor of the Illinois State Museum.
- **1948:** Continuation of the 1947 work under Orr and McGregor on Starved Rock.
- **1949:** Continuation of work under Orr and McGregor and excavations conducted under the auspices of the Illinois department of Public Works and Buildings by Archaeologist Richard Hagen.
- **1950:** Continuation of Richard Hagen's work on the summit of Starved Rock.
- **1974:** Excavations by a team from the University of Illinois

Chicago under Robert Hall.

- **1981:** Excavations by a team under the supervision of Ed Jelks, from the Midwest Archaeological Research Center at Illinois State University to investigate area of the proposed wooden walkway.

Appendix B

The following is a list of Starved Rock State Park Custodians/Site Superintendents

- Alexander Richards
- Peter Henry Harbeck
- J.P. White
- James Williams
- George Malone
- Terry Martin
- John Biggs
- J. Heitman
- Jack Querciagrossa
- Dominic Costello
- John Blume
- Bob Kleczewski
- Tom Levy

Park Naturalists/Site Interpreters

- Dr. Donald Ries
- Robert T. Burns
- Mike Winter
- Debbie Raymond

- Tobias Miller

Starved Rock Hotel and Lodge Concessionaires

- Charles Touton
- W.E. Crosier
- Nick Spiros
- George Spiros
- Josephine Schmidt
- Terry Cross and John Reilly
- Terry Cross

Illinois Conservation Police Officers who were assigned to La Salle County and Starved Rock State Park

- Phillip Cole
- Dave Charles
- Ken Swiderski
- Mark Walczynski
- Greg Hunter
- Scott Travi
- Eric Anderson
- Brian McReynolds
- Chad Compton
- Jeffrey Lane
- Phillip Wire
- Joseph Kaufman

Appendix C

Dates of Importance Associated with the History of Starved Rock and the Illinois Department of Natural Resources

- 1673 French explorers Jacques Marquette and Louis Jolliet are the first Europeans to see Starved Rock.
- 1680 Explorer La Salle makes the first historical reference to Starved Rock.
- 1682-1683 (winter) Fort Saint-Louis is built on Starved Rock: The fort on Starved Rock becomes headquarters of "La Salle's Colony."
- 1683 First land grant awarded in Illinois by explorer La Salle to Jacques Bourdon d'Autray. The grant encompassed most of today's Starved Rock State Park.
- 1684 Starved Rock is besieged for six days by an Iroquois war party.
- 1691 Fort Saint-Louis is abandoned by the French when the Illinois tribes relocate to Lake Peoria and later, the Mississippi River in Southern Illinois.
- 1710 New Englander Joseph Kellogg passes Starved Rock while en route to the Mississippi River.
- 1721 the French Jesuit writer Charlevoix visits Starved Rock.

- 1722 Peoria Indians on Plum Island are attacked by the Fox Indians and are besieged on the summit of Starved Rock.
- 1769 Ottawa Chief Pontiac is killed in Cahokia, Illinois by an Illinois Indian. Contrary to the famous legend, his death was NOT followed by the destruction of Illinois Indians at the Rock.
- 1773 Patrick Kennedy leads a British geological expedition past Starved Rock.
- 1789 American expedition maps the Illinois River and notes "Small Rocks," today's Starved Rock.
- 1821 Henry Schoolcraft visits Starved Rock while awaiting horses to travel to Chicago. He notes his observations of the site.
- 1834 The first historical reference to the name "Starved Rock."
- 1835 Daniel Hitt purchases Starved Rock from the U.S. Government.
- 1873 Two-hundredth year pageant commemorating the voyage of Marquette and Jolliet held at Starved Rock.
- 1885 First Illinois Game Wardens hired.
- 1889 First Illinois Fish Warden hired.
- 1890 Hitt sells Starved Rock to Starved Rock businessman Ferdinand Walther.
- 1891 Starved Rock Hotel is built.
- 1903 Illinois Game Commission formed-wardens worked under it.
- 1911 Starved Rock becomes Illinois' second state park.
- 1912 Film companies make movies at the park.
- 1913 Illinois Game and Fish Commission formed-Fish and Game Wardens merged.
- 1917 Illinois Game and Fish Commission merged into the Department of Agriculture.
- 1918 One-hundredth anniversary of Illinois statehood celebrated at Starved Rock.
- 1925 Illinois Department of Conservation formed.
- 1933 Starved Rock Lock and Dam completed
- 1933-1937 Part of the Starved Rock Lodge built by the Civilian Conservation Corps.
- 1938 First park naturalist hired
- 1939 Starved Rock Lodge opened.

- 1940 Starved Rock Hotel demolished.
- 1942 State of Illinois acquires today's Matthiessen State Park
- 1951 Division of Parks and Memorials transferred to the Illinois Department of Conservation.
- 1960 Three women murdered in Saint Louis Canyon.
- 1962 Today's Utica bridge built and west park entrance road improved and completed.
- 1967 The Starved Rock Nature Preserve donated to the State of Illinois and the land becomes the eighteenth dedicated nature preserve in Illinois.
- 1972 Illinois Department of Conservation Inspectors become the Illinois Conservation Police
- 1975 Airplane rides on Plum Island discontinued.
- 1975 Starved Rock Campground moved to East 950th Road. Additional properties donated to Starved State Park (west of Illinois Route 178)
- 1981 New wooden walkway constructed on the summit of Starved Rock
- 1982 Overlooks built on Lover's Leap, Eagle Cliff, Owl Canyon, Hennepin Canyon, and Beehive Rock.
- 1988-1989 Major Lodge renovation and new parking lot built.
- 1995 Department of Conservation becomes the Department of Natural Resources.
- 1997-1999 Three phase construction project completed. 1) Wooden staircase (Jacob's ladder) built to south summit of Lover's Leap Bluff; 2) wooden walkway built that connects Jacob's ladder to Lover's Leap and Eagle Cliff overlooks; 3) shoreline stabilization completed.
- 2000 Whitetail deer season opens at Starved Rock and Matthiessen State Parks.
- 2002 New Visitor's center opened to the public.
- 2009 Starved Rock State Park voted one of the Seven Wonders of Illinois.
- 2011 Starved Rock celebrates 100 years as an Illinois State Park.

Sources

Clarence Alvord and Clarence Carter, "Trade and Politics: 1767-1769" *Collections of the Illinois Historical Library*, vol. XVI, 1921: Springfield, Illinois).

Elmer T. Baldwin *History of La Salle County, Illinois* (1877: Rand, McNally, & Co., Chicago).

Joseph F. Booton, "How the Lodge Came to Starved Rock," *Illinois Public Works* (1945).

John Dean Caton. *The Last of the Illinois and A Sketch of the Pottawatomies* (Chicago: Rand McNally & Co., 1870).

Helen Martin Donovan, *Starved Rock Legendary* (O'Donnell Printing Co., 1915: Chicago).

Judith A. Franke, *French Peoria and the Illinois Country 1673-1846*, Illinois State Museum Popular Sciences Series, vol. XII, (1995: State Museum Society, Springfield, IL.).

Richard S. Hagen, *Progress Report of the Archaeological Research at Starved Rock State Park La Salle County, Illinois,* 1950.

Robert L. Hall, "The Archaeology of La Salle's Fort St. Louis on Starved Rock and the Problem of the Newell Fort," in John A. Walthall, (ed.) *French Colonial Archaeology* (1991: University of Illinois Press).

Edward B. Jelks (ed.), *Archaeological Explorations at Starved Rock,*

Illinois (11LS12). Report prepared for the Illinois Department of Conservation by the Midwestern Archaeological Research Center, (1982: Normal, Illinois: Illinois State University.

Louis Phelps Kellogg (ed.), "Memoirs on La Salle's Discoveries, by Tonty, 1678-1690 [1693] in *Early Narratives of the Northwest, 1634-1699*, (2001 Heritage Books reprint of 1917 work, Bowie, Maryland).

John C. McGregor and Kenneth G. Orr, *Archaeological Excavations Near Starved Rock, Progress Report 1947* (May 1948).

Kenneth G. Orr, *Summary Statements of the Present Status of Archaeological Research in the Starved Rock Area, La Salle County, Illinois* (June, 1949).

Eda K. Pegram, Ceremonies at Starved Rock, *Daughters of the American Revolution Magazine*, Vol. XLIV, No.1 (1913: New York).

Report of the Illinois Park Commission of the State of Illinois (1912).

John, Reynolds, *Pioneer History of Illinois Containing the Discovery in 1673 and the History of the Country to the Year 1818 When State Government was Organized* (1968 reprint of 1852 work, Xerox).

Gail Schroeder Schnell (ed.), "Hotel Plaza: An Early Historic Site with a Long Prehistory," *Illinois State Museum Reports of Investigations,* no. 29, (1974: Springfield, IL).

Reuben Gold Thwaites (ed.), *Wisconsin Historical Collections,* vol. XVI (1902: State Historical Society of Wisconsin, Madison).

Reuben Gold Thwaites (ed.), *Jesuit Relations and Allied Documents 1610-1791.* (1901: Cleveland).

Unpublished reports of Richard Hagen to Joseph F. Booton, Chief of Design, Illinois Dept. of Public Works and Buildings, Division of Architecture and Engineering

Newspapers

- Streator Times Press
- Chicago Tribune
- La Salle Post Tribune
- La Salle Daily Tribune

- Princeton Republican
- Rock Island Argus
- Illinois State Journal
- Chicago Tribune
- Ottawa Free Trader-Journal
- Ottawa Daily Republican Times
- Peru Daily News Herald
- Illinois Times
- Danville Community News
- Minonk Dispatch

Miscellaneous Correspondences

- Robert Kingery to George Malone
- Robert Kingery to James Williams
- H.H. Cleaveland to John Boyle
- John Boyle to H.H. Cleaveland
- Governor Emmerson to H.H. Cleaveland
- H.H. Cleaveland to Harold Watson
- H.H. Cleaveland to Governor Emmerson
- H.H. Cleaveland to Walter Fox
- H.H. Cleaveland to Edmond P. Conerton
- W.C. Jones to Harold G. Watson
- US Congressman John T. Buckbee to John G. Boyle
- Daniel Sullivan to Robert Kingery
- Robert Kingery to Chicago Tribune
- Paul M. Angle to Robert Kingery
- Baugy to La Durantaye (1684)
- Robert Kingery to Paul M. Angle

CPSIA information can be obtained at www.ICGtesting.com
Printed in the USA
LVOW07s1140050315

429352LV00033BA/802/P

9 781432 776107